Between You,
Me and
the Gatepost

ALSO BY PAT BOONE:

'Twixt Twelve and Twenty

Between You, Me and the Gatepost

by

PAT BOONE

PRENTICE-HALL, INC., Englewood Cliffs, N. J.

Contents

Coming Attractions

Hi, _____! Please fill in your name like before.

Maybe you've noticed that most books have an Introduction?

Well, this one hasn't!

However . . . before we jump barefooted into the next 50,000 words (give or take a dangling participle or two), I think we oughta get a couple of things straight and set our sights.

First of all, I know you and you know me. I know what you think about most things (I haven't forgotten) and you're pretty well acquainted with my thought processes, too. In short order, we'll know each other a lot better.

Why a new book? That's a good question. I've said many times since *'Twixt Twelve and Twenty* that the first one took me 24 years to write and I didn't see another in my near future. I thought we covered everything I had to say the first time around, but your letters have doubled since then and I find many areas we didn't touch that you're very interested in. Secondly, I guess we just skimmed over some of the things that had you "hung up" the most, and *you let me know it!*

So okay. Fine. "If you got the money, honey, I got the time," like the song says. And as the Kingston Trio once remarked (they were on an album cover at the time), HERE WE GO AGAIN!

Mainly, what you want to know is:

> *How can I make the most of today?*
> *How can I get ready to make the most of tomorrow?*

Check? Check. We'll give those questions the best answers we can scrape up. On top of that, I've got some ideas for you on how you—yes, *you*—can have a big influence on our country and our world right now! You're not too young this very minute, and I hope to prove it to you.

We'll also talk about opening oysters. But wait till we get to Chapter Three for that.

I've worked like Bugs Bunny in a carrot patch digging up answers for "hot potatoes" like these that were hurled at me recently during a teenage journalist's conference in New York (arranged by the Ladies' Home Journal):

Is the steeple being replaced by the nose cone? (In other words, is God losing ground in the Space Age?)

Are teen-agers today losing their identity?

Are you really having it softer than mom and dad did?

Is it good or bad for teen-agers to model themselves after entertainers and stars instead of some more worth-while goal? (And me an entertainer!)

Have teen-age morals and ethical values degenerated, and if so, are rock 'n roll, movies, advertising, vicious literature, etc., a determining factor? (Wow! To ask this of a paid professional singer!— But I told you—for you I'll brave it!)

Can teen-agers themselves dispel the resentment and rebellion that causes adult restrictions and punishments?

To what do I attribute juvenile delinquency? Is the punishment severe enough for the offenses? Would a curfew law help?

What was my opinion of teen-agers going steady? Does it help or hinder their lives?

Considering the headlines about teen-age violence caused by about three per cent of the teen-agers, how can the rest of us counteract the bad publicity? How can we get newspapers to publicize the good side of teen-age activities?

How can you best handle the accelerated high school programs demanded of many of you today and learn to accept higher challenges and lower grades?

Do I think parents of today show enough sense of responsibility toward their children? Do I think teen-agers show enough responsibility toward their parents?

Verily I say unto thee, . . . woweeWOOwow! You think my work's not cut out for me? And these weren't adults asking the questions; no sir . . . these were bonafide, picked-at-random TWEEN-AGERS!

Now, here's what we'll do: *First,* we'll talk about YOU; *Second,* about you and your friends (including parents!); and *Third,* about the ways you, Egbert Z. Twixt, can meet the challenge of changing the world!

Big talk? Let's see if I can make it stick.

You're constantly attacked and challenged as a generation, as a group. And you as an individual answer, sometimes wistfully, sometimes defiantly, *"What can I do?"* And that big question is exactly what we are going to talk about.

Pull up a comfy seat, a King-size Coke, and let's yak. This is gonna be a personal, private jam session just "between you, me and the gatepost."

Now you get the title, right?

Your boy,

PAT BOONE

Cooga Mooga, N.Y.

1

The Importance of Being You

"They tool up their cars with triple carburetors, blast off to the drag strip, eat fried broccoli sandwiches, and drink Coke mixed with ginger ale. They like the lights low, the tempo hot, a real 'bop beat' . . . They cut their hair flattop, or pony-tail style, wear leotards and button-down sports shirts, trade bobby pins and football letters when they're going steady. It's Zorch! It's crazy! It's teen-age life."

Recognize *you*—the "typical" teen-ager—in that picture? Or have you taken a good look at yourself lately?

Newsweek magazine *did* take a look at you in an article called "Our *Good* Teen-Agers"[1] from which the above is quoted. However, as he eyed you "through the looking-glass" of his article, the writer seemed to see two images—both you!

One is of a generation "reckless, apathetic, conformist, immature . . . blown completely out of control."

The other image, expressed by a respected California high school principal is that you're "as fine a generation as the world has ever known."

So who's confused? Not me! You kiddin'? I agree whole-

[1] *Newsweek*—Special Education Report—Nov. 23, 1959.

heartedly with the high school principal—always have. When I'm asked if I think you're "reckless" or "out of control" as a generation, I confidently say "What, me worry?" (Gets a big reaction.)

Not only don't I worry, but I'll go a step further. I think it's mighty important to me, the country, and most of all to *you,* that you go right on being—YOU. As a generation, and as individuals.

But one bearded cynic who actually felt many of you don't *know* what you want and wouldn't like it if you got it, used this illustration of the little boy who wouldn't eat. His mother went to see a specialist when junior's hunger strike got out of hand and was advised to humor him in every possible way, including getting him any odd type food his little tummy rumbled for. So the first thing junior demanded was a fish-worm.

His mother shuddered and dutifully went out and hunted up a fish-worm.

"I want it cooked," junior said firmly.

So mama fried it in butter.

"Okay," said mamma's little man, "you eat your half and I'll eat mine."

His long suffering mother duly choked down a piece of fish-worm whereupon junior shrieked, "OOoow, you ate my half!"

The moral of this story, the gentleman pointed out, was that since young people today get too much too easily they not only don't know what they want nor like what they get, but such a "spoiled" and "flabby" generation is soft. It won't develop the moral muscles of those youngsters of the past who had to fight for every fish-worm and eat it raw.

Am I an Optimist? I hope so. The definition of an Optimist is—a Hope Addict. But in this case it isn't blind hope. I'm betting on a sure thing and I can prove it. Don't forget, I *know* you. And I know that when you read all these conflicting judgments, and you *do* read 'em!—you get a little shook. Who wouldn't? You say wistfully, your soda straws falling into your lap, "Are we so different? Are we so far off the beam?" And then you ask, puzzled, "If not, when grown-ups look at us, *how* can some of them see us good and some see us bad?"

By George, I think I've got it! I think there are two reasons. One is that some of them don't remember. The other is that some of them don't understand.

Darling Do You Remember When . . . ?

Of course, *you* don't remember. And neither do *I* . . . not this far back. But I've just finished pounding some history books and I find that the only reason you're different from other teen-age generations is because you're actually the same! By nature, that is. Each healthy new younger crop seems to want to trade in the customs and traditions of the last one and find some new expressions of its own, a word or phrase, a sandwich, a haircut, or a style in dress. I know that six or seven years ago we wouldn't have dreamed of eating broccoli sandwiches! Onion-burgers were *our* style.

Half a century ago the pulpit and press were in a *sweat* about the spreading fad for "ragtime." In that day another news magazine reported for the raised eyebrow brigade such slang phrases as "Flossy. Beat it! Peeved! Classy. Fussed. Nutty. Peachy. Getting your goat. It's a cinch! (So it isn't Zorch?)."

Skip twenty years. What do we see? A "rebellious generation" which was also in some ways "Lost" whooping it up with bloomers and "plus-fours" for sports, wide trousers and raccoon coats for the dating boy, short skirts, long waist lines and fringe for the belles. I'm glad I missed all that stuff.

Although I do remember a pair of "real cool" green pants I bought as a freshman in H.S. I figgered they were sure-fire lady-killers! I strutted down the hall between classes, just knowing that the girls were swooning into their lockers. In fact, I was *so* confident of my sartorial splendor that it took

me quite a while to figure out why every time I'd "con-
descend" to speak to one of the prettier young ladies, she'd
seem to remember some private joke and break out giggling!
Well, I'm slow, but not stupid—pretty soon I got a hunch
what that "private joke" was all about. So my treasured green
trousers became my favorite milking pants! Rosemary, our
cow, never laughed. She tried to *eat* 'em, but she never
laughed.

I guess those green pants just came along too late—they
belonged to the "Lost Generation" of twenty years before!

Fortunately, enough of this Lost Generation was "Found"
in time to become very good parents to my own. And fortunately for us, too, a big lot of *Parents* and even *Grandparents* do remember.

I just had a wonderful experience. I went fishing with my
Granddaddy Pritchard, down in Jacksonville, Fla. We'd been
talking about it for years, and finally got around to it. He's a
handsome, tall, white-haired, salty old (80) builder and
politician. "Mr. Pritch" is a "big cheese" down at City Hall,
where he's still going strong as City Maintenance Supervisor.
I and the rest of his grandchildren have always loved him,
but I got to know him a little better on this fishing trip.

As we sat in the old boat, watching the little cork bob
lightly on the water, Granddaddy told me stories about his
own boyhood that I'd never heard before. Why, he was a regular Tom Sawyer when he was a kid! I mean a real rascal! He
was always sneaking off from home and smoking raw to-
bacco with the hired hands and swiping watermelons and
raisin' all kinds o' Cain!

No wonder there was always a mysterious twinkle in his
eye when Nick, my brother, and I got into some kind of mischief during our Summer visits in Jacksonville. Oh, he
scolded us, and even occasionally had to punish us, and we
had a healthy respect for that big mitt of his. But somehow,
that twinkle in his eye told us that he understood, and wasn't
too worried about us. Now I understand that he knew he'd

probably have been in the same jam with us if he were our age. Your Granddad's the same way, I'll bet.

These "old folks" seem to stay more pliable, more closely in touch with their own youth through us. And they're less fearful of our odder symptoms— (all right, c'mon, you know a flattop *is* odd;—neat—but odd!). The best parents have a visual memory of their own teen years, plus a sense of humor. With this equipment they can see the true picture and distinguish accurately between harmless originality—and harmful recklessness and self-will.

After all, let's not kid ourselves. There is always the chance of over-doing things, or doing the wrong things, or even doing the right things in the wrong way. Right?

A percentage of each succeeding Younger Generation (a small one) will carry matters to an extreme—and that's bad. A percentage (a small one) will violate laws, both human and Divine. And that's sad, both for them as individuals, and for the rest of their age group (because they get a *lot* of publicity, all the wrong kind).

Now. 'Nuff said. Let's get to the point.

The fact that every normal new generation decides "what was good enough for mom and dad isn't good enough for me" is a pretty favorable sign. What's wrong with that?

You do more than reflect the old—the world of today. You begin to form the new—the world of tomorrow.

This is the *importance of being you.*

For this reason the goals you develop are of vital concern to all of us. We're gonna talk a lot about those goals.

But for now, do me a favor. If you suffer today from unjust criticism, well, twenty years after the day after tomorrow, when *you're* the parent of a teen-ager (and you will be), make it *your* job *to remember!*

You remember that each succeeding generation is gonna try for its own expression of the *same* things—they'll want to use their own pep and vitality, and joy at just being young and alive, to create fashions and styles and language and music of their own, exactly as *yours* has done. You'll know it isn't rebellion. It isn't being "out of control." Don't let it ever frighten you. That is, *if* it rests on a solid foundation of moral and spiritual values, sound aims and goals, the *right ingredients* for the teen-ager to express in his own individual way.

Don't you dare say, "What? They eat chopped petunia sandwiches? For Pete's sake! What *are* they coming to?"

But, "Chopped petunia; hmmmm? Well, it's kooky, but it doesn't violate any principles. And it just may be a sign of progress. Because I seem to remember (and you don't *have* to say this out loud) that broccoli sandwiches were good enough for us!"

Do You Understand You?

Now we come around to the question of who understands whom.

We've been talking about "you" as a group—now let's "zoom in" to a closeup of *"you"*—the individual.

We've had a description of "you" from the outside as a "typical" teen-ager. Well, maybe *you're* not so "typical." So we're going to look inside.

And maybe, for a couple minutes, you're not gonna be very happy with me. Sure, I'm well aware that a lot of grownups don't understand you either as a group *or* as an individual, inside or outside—(either because they've got short memories or feel they're too old). But—I think it's high time to stop passing the buck. I don't think *you* always understand *you* either (because you're too young, maybe. . . . But never too young to start trying!)

This puts me in an enviable position because I'm not too young. I'm not too old. I'm in-between. So I *do* understand. And I *do* remember. And I *am* going to be honest with you.

If you're anything like my buddies and I were, well, I can let you in on something. There were times when we weren't too sure what we were all about. Are you always? Honestly? If not, why not? Glad you asked—I'll tell you. Because you're in a state of transition. You're just in second gear. You're rarely the same today as you were yesterday and you may not even be the same this minute as you were sixty seconds ago. And that takes a lot of understanding.

You don't believe me? So I'll explain. You are, at this moment, an emotional and psychological and physical phenomenon (I'll bet you've never been called *that* before) experiencing the various stages of a metamorphosis (tighten your seat belt), trying to achieve maturity in an eight-year period. You can see where all that might add up to a large experience. I didn't copy it out of Webster's dictionary It seeped into my noggin in college.

Don't let it fog you, though. Reduced to simple jive, a metamorphosis is nothing more nor less than a complete change in character, purpose, and responsibilities, a passing from one form into another without a change of nature (You'll still come out you—but different—follow me?). A caterpillar manages all this very spectacularly when it goes into its cocoon a lowly crawler and emerges as a magnificent but probably very surprised flying garden ornament.

We, the human animals, go into the teens as carefree, dependent children with clearly defined rules and limitations. Then from twelve to twenty we accomplish the change into high flying, independent adults whose boundaries are infinity, and whose responsibilities are great.

We're not like the cartoon that's always tickled me that pictures a fella on the street meeting up with a young lady he hasn't seen since they were children. "Why, Gladys!" he says, "the last time I saw you, you were just a skinny, freckle-faced, awkward little girl in pigtails!" And there she stands now—a skinny, freckle-faced, awkward BIG girl in pigtails.

No, we're not like that. We change.

Unfortunately, you can't go into a sleepy cocoon and emerge with the transformation already complete. You have to do it the hard way, on stage, front and center, because only your body makes the change automatically. For the rest, the psychological and emotional changes required of you, it's necessary that you explore your environment, make social experiments, test, accept, reject, succeed, fail, adjust, readjust. In short, you "try your wings," build your confidence and self-esteem until you can really fly alone. In these struggles you're bound to come into conflict with your surroundings. So one minute you're Joan of Arc and the next the Incredible Shrinking Man—trying to fit in.

Teeners have new impulses—and these require new controls and special handling. It's like switching over from Piper Cub to Jet. We develop the controls and seem very grown-up and then suddenly they slip a little and we're not grown-up at all. Like the guy whose voice is changing, who jabbers in deep masculine tones that continue to surprise and delight him——except at those horrifying moments when it gets all out of control and he sounds like Lily Pons with a bad cold.

Another thing, we suddenly find we're becoming responsible for steering our own boats a little. Where once Mom or Dad made the decisions for us, now we feel the need to make a few for ourselves. At first we love the taste of it. But it's possible to take the wrong turn now and then.

We can find ourselves in the position of the husky young man who took a job on a farm and amazed the ol' farmer by the amount of work he did. In one morning he pulled up all the tree stumps in a useless field and in the same afternoon he plowed it. He dug irrigation ditches ceaselessly with the speed of a human mole and always he asked for more work. Finally the farmer, afraid of losing this gem, decided to give him an easier job for a day or two and set him in the barn sorting seed potatoes. All the hired man had to do was sit on a stool, watch the potatoes come down the chute, pick out the best ones for seed and drop them in a basket.

After one day of this he quit. The farmer was amazed. "What's the trouble," he demanded. "Be I workin' ye too hard?"

"Not yesterday," the young man said, "nor t' day before that, but *today*. There I sit all day long—makin' decisions —decisions—*decisions*. That be too hard for any one man alone."

And so the teen-ager finds it.

All of this is a pretty tall order for us humans at the early stages. It takes some learnin' as well as doin'. We can use help. And there's help available all over, a lot of it—which we'll discuss in due time. But when we first find we can't handle it alone we often try conforming to the pack, or crowd, or club, or whatever. Then *it* makes decisions for us. We feel safe if "all the others" do it. But this is only good if the crowd has high ideals and sound principles. (And that's a rare bird, Jim.) And it is only good *until* such time as we come to understand ourselves. If we hang on too long we *do* become conformists. We're sheep willing to follow wherever we're led.

And who wants to be a sheep?

The day we really begin to grow up is that day when we begin to make consistent decisions for ourselves—and that day can be *today* and that moment can be *now!*

Are Teen-Agers of Today Losing Their Identity?

Again I say a confident "No!"

Your identity, your individuality, can't be lost. Every single one of your 18,000,000 personalities (and there are about eighteen million of you today from thirteen to nineteen) is unique. The Bible says even the hairs of our head are numbered—and science agrees that no two of *them* are alike. Nor your finger prints nor your voice, face, nor your thoughts, talents or aims.

You are *you*—and there will never be another one like you! Your kid brother will be happy to hear *that*.

But I will say this:

You do not begin to show your individuality, or identity,

you will not begin to be "grown up," until you're willing to leave the temporary security of the crowd and find out who *you* are—and what *you* think—and what *your* talents are.

Now I've told you how I feel about the "typical" teen-ager. I remember. I understand. And as a whole, a group, a generation, you *do* have great importance and impact and I think you're good for what ails us.

But you'll never attain your individual importance in the scheme of things until you have ceased to be a "typical" anything!

You will never be completely accepted as a *You*, a person distinct from a group, until you have the courage to abandon the accepted group rules and customs if you discover better ones of your own.

And, oh friend, it does take courage!

We'd never have had David slaying Goliath with his stone-age U-2 rocket, nor Joan of Arc saving France, nor Lindbergh flying the Atlantic, if these young people had decided to sit back safely and do what everybody else did! And remember, David and Joan were teen-agers!

In some ways the not-quite-so-popular teen-ager who walks alone, thinks alone, and prays some too, is more apt to blossom out earlier with a definite personality and identity than the kid who's huddling in the security and conformity of the social group.

A case in point that I've always remembered was the early life of the beloved motion-picture and TV personality, Zasu Pitts.

When she was thirteen, Zasu was all the things a girl just entering the teen-age doesn't want to be; shy, awkward, scrawny. Her spare time was spent cooking, scrubbing, washing, helping her widowed mother who ran a rooming house. Zasu wore hand-me-downs, never could have a party, didn't have a "chum."

Today, if we didn't call her "under-privileged" the kindest

thing we could say would be that as a child she had "no advantages."

And what was worse, she was constantly subjected to ridicule. Boys sent her comic valentines, pulled her pig-tails and jeered at her— "Boo—hoo—Za-su . . . Monkey face, from a zoo!"

The girls giggled and the boys taunted . . . and there was no security in "the crowd," no chance of conforming, for this bewildered, hurt, teen-ager.

Zasu didn't cry to anyone—not even her mother—but she did pray.

Then one day she made a friend, no less a personage than the principal of the school, a man who both remembered and understood the pain that can come to an awkward adolescent, and she confided to him her one big dream, the dream she had never even told her mother—the one thing she really longed to do was a dramatic reading of "The Midnight Ride of Paul Revere" on Graduation Day.

You know that the principal, even with deep concern over the outcome, granted her wish.

You know the triumph she dreamed of—the smashing success that would follow her dramatic recital.

And you know what happened.

When Zasu Pitts, in her same old hand-me-down gingham, stood forth to recite—they *laughed*. She tried again. Her voice squeaked and trailed off. And they *laughed*. She waved a hand helplessly—and they fell in the aisle.

Stunned, white, too shaken for tears, Zasu stumbled into the wings. And the audience clamored for MORE.

"Go back and finish," said the principal, "they love you!"

"They're laughing at me," she wailed.

"They're laughing *with* you. Maybe that's your mission in life," said this wise man. "Maybe that's what God intended, and His wisdom is greater than ours! Laughter," he whispered when the little girl still hesitated—lacking courage to trade in the vision of herself as a great dramatic actress, sensitive to the pain of being laughed at, afraid to play the clown, "Laughter is God's hand upon a troubled world."

And so Zasu Pitts, in that minute, found her identity—her talent, her purpose. She had the courage to step back on that stage and *be herself*.

In later chapters, particularly Chapter Three, we'll dig into some detailed methods for finding your own talents and identity. It has to do with opening oysters, remember?

But make up your mind now that the *most important person* in the whole world for you to be is *you*. You have something unique and wonderful and God-given to contribute to life.

The oyster you want to open is *your own*.

The pearl you will find will be unlike all others. And your joy will be in sharing it or giving it to the world.

2

The Magic within You

Ron Walsher and I have been kind of co-teachers of the teen-age Sunday School class at Manhattan Church of Christ (48 East 80th—come see us). Ron works for the U.S. Health Service on the side, and is quite a guy. He was talking about this talent and abilities situation the other morning and the class (all real wits) were giving him a hard time in a good natured way. Over their comments and wisecracks, Ron was saying that each of us has some special ability. "There is *something* that *you* can do better than anybody in your class—."

"I'm in a very big class," chirped up Wes Johnson, Jr.

Quick as a wink, Ron said, "I'll bet you're better at 'wising off' than *any* of 'em, Wes!"

He'd made his point. I'll bet somebody told Bob Hope that once, and he took it seriously! He made a career of it—and a great one

Every one of us has something unique and wonderful and God-given—remember? We don't know yet exactly what we'll give to the world but there are no limits to the possibilities.

There was a conversation at Scout camp once where a thirteen-year-old put this idea into simple words. He had refused point blank to learn to darn his socks because it—oh, I don't know—I guess he thought it was beneath his dignity. "Look," said his leader, "George Washington did his own sewing in the wars. Do you think you're better than George Washington?"

"I don't know yet," said the boy. "Only time will tell."

He was right. Only time—plus the decisions we make—can tell what we will become. And his decision was that he wasn't going to darn socks even to become like the Father of his Country.

But I think most of us, in our inside hearts (the "you" that lives in "your house"), want to be something great and do noble deeds. Why, I was a Hero in every one of my teendreams! Imagine! And I haven't made it yet. But I'll clue you. You don't quit dreaming when you reach age 20. We all share visions of what great deeds we'd do if faced with the unexpected—an earthquake, a firing squad, a kid crying in a burning house, a chance to bat in the World Series with two out and the bases loaded, a prowler while we're baby-sitting, an overturned canoe on a moonlit lake.

Only rarely does some such excitement come our way. But daily we're faced, instead, with a series of less dramatic emergencies—like running out of cornflakes in the morning —which still demand quick decisions and sound reactions! Just crossing any busy intersection on foot, f'r instance, is a real hair-raising adventure these days.

But more important, and more dramatic, are the moral and ethical emergencies that face us as we start through the teens. These demand more difficult decisions. "Should I let Johnny kiss me?" or "Is anything wrong with just *borrowing* this for a while?" or "Should I tell the folks what *really* happened?" Your answers to questions like these will decide whether you're a Hero or a flop *today,* and whether your special abilities will have the chance to make you an important person *tomorrow*. Your answers *now* will determine who you are in the future! Get the point?

I goofed so many times that it's a wonder I'm anybody at all. But Mama and Daddy picked me up every time I fell in the early teens and I had plenty of help from other sources later on. Eventually I got to where I could make up my own mind and half-way expect it to turn out O.K. As far as the ethical decisions of dating are concerned, I'm glad that I dated good girls. This meant that I didn't have to always depend on just my own moral strength. Believe me, a date whose principles are showing can make your private tussles with yourself a lot easier to win.

Sometimes a step in the wrong direction teaches you the importance of keeping your feet where they belong. When I was a sophomore, there was a beautiful blonde freshman who started her high school career with a pretty hot reputation already cooking. In spite of this, I asked her for a date. We wound up in the back seat of a friend's car, on a moonlit night, parked on a bridge overlooking a little waterfall. We talked, we kidded—we kissed. It could have become a very dangerous situation, but for one thing. The girl in the *front* seat was different from the one in back. She pretty single-handedly kept the atmosphere light and clean by chatting and avoiding clinches.

As we drove home, I couldn't help comparing the two gals, and by the time we delivered them to the girls' dorm I was convinced I should have been with the front seat doll. I felt sort of sneaky and cheap with my date, and although she soon grew out of this stage she was in, I never had any desire to go out with her again. On the other hand, it was a while before I could get up the guts to ask the Young Lady for a date.

Are Teen-Age Morals Slipping?

Gradually, I think they are. But the young people are not alone. So are the morals and ethics of their elders! In fact, how *can* a young person grow up with a clean mind and good standards these days when he's constantly surrounded by suggestive and violent movies and TV shows, sex-filled magazines, and a general adult preoccupation with money, possessions, position, and questionable entertainment? So I sound like a preacher? Well, my good friend, we need a lot of preaching right now if we're going to keep this country and its people what they ought to be!

Fifty years ago there was no such thing as a "teen-ager!" I mean, a girl in her teen years was sheltered and chaperoned till she was an adult. A young fella was really still considered a child 'til he finished school, and had very few important decisions to make until he was suddenly on his own! Parents, teachers, chaperones and all kinds of authorities kept the young person in check all the time and made most of his "habits" for him.

Today, such a short time later, it makes me sick at heart to see panels of teen-agers *on TV* discussing petting, necking, delinquency and worse things. You have to decide for *yourself* while you've still got diaper rash what kind of person you're gonna be, whether you'll get home on time or into trouble, whether you'll cheat or flunk, whether you should get married now or wait till you get out of *high school!*

But that's the way it is. What're we gonna do about it?

Be-Prepared Magic:

Now—how can a teen-ager be prepared to make the right decision on any matter, whether the spectacular, front-page type challenge calling for heroism, or the ordinary ones that crop up in your letters like "What to do 'til the doctor comes" or "is this boy too old for me like my mom says?" or the ethical and moral ones like "is parking all right if you like a boy real well" or "will it do any harm if I copy Jane's homework this once, because I'm failing?" How can you have any kind of mature judgment with so little experience? How can you do it—because you *must!*

Well, I know of only one Common Denominator that will give us the courage and wisdom to decide ninety per cent of 'em, and when we give it wings, it'll decide the other ten per cent.

I can *tell* you this C.D. in two words—I can't *give* it to you at all. I only wish I could, 'cause if I could dip my hand into a big jar of it, I'd keep a liberal dose for myself! I could use some more! But it has to be individually learned and earned. It's another "do-it-yourself" deal. With it you have a magic formula to apply to emergencies large and small plus a sound daily guide for solving almost any problem for yourself. Without it, you can stop even dreaming of "How To Be A Hero." Forget it, Charlie.

The two words that wrap up this preparedness magic are —Common Sense.

Does that sound like a drag? Let's check it. First let's hear from a hero. A real one.

The Duke of Wellington, the very same old Iron Duke who handed Napoleon his Waterloo, was once complimented on his military brilliance during an earlier campaign in India. He brushed aside the laurels and said that, at that time, he was simply acting on the conclusion that there must be a crossing at a particular point of a river because there he saw two villages on opposite sides of it. "That," he added, "is *common sense.* And when one is strongly intent on an object, common sense will usually direct one to the right means."

See? Here a genuine, time-tested hero shrugs off Brilliance and claims Common Sense and in the process makes an inspired victory look simple. And this same Common Denominator pokes a hole in the magic of the magician!

Take the case of a marvelous prophet who displeased Tiberius Caesar when Rome was ruling the world, by prophesying uncomplimentary things about the Emperor. Now the

wrath of Caesar could kick up quite a storm and our poor
old stargazer found himself before the Emperor and his entire court——sentenced to be thrown from a cliff and dashed
to death in the rocky sea below. The soothsayer heard his
fate calmly, then stepped close to Caesar and murmured a
few quiet words in his ear. Their effect was startling. Immediately the death sentence was lifted and from that moment everything possible was done to pamper and preserve
the man formerly condemned. Rome was agog. What spell,
what incantation had bewitched the great Caesar? It looked
like strong magic. Yet it was so simple. All the soothsayer
had done was make another prophecy.

"My death," he whispered, "will take place three days before your majesty's."

Quick witted? Yes. Magic? No. Only the magic of Common
Sense. For if the soothsayer didn't want to die, well, neither
did the Emperor. The trick was to find a way to get this
across and, as the Iron Duke pointed out, "when one is
strongly intent on an object (like not getting spread on the
rocks) common sense will usually direct one to the right
means."

What, exactly, is Common Sense?

It's just good, plain, logical *thinking*—founded on observation, information, and or experience. Now you take these and
add one more quality and you have the brand that originated
in America, that makes America and Americans what they
are—the greatest. *Common Sense plus Humor equals Horse
Sense.* And that's the American heritage and the American
ideal!

The Homespun Philosopher, the Cracker Barrel Wit
(you know, the old 'kook' sitting by the stove in the country
store spouting 'goodies' and 'popping cornies') are uniquely
American. Their Common Sense philosophy dates from the
very time of our Independence when Benjamin Franklin
had already launched it in *Poor Richard's Almanac* (my favorite of this deceased expert is the one where Poor Richard

anticipated the modern Rush-Rush by announcing: "He who riseth late, must trot all day.") down to today—when the definition of Hoss Sense is that it's "what keeps hosses from betting on people." And right now, I'd like to throw my hat in the Cracker Barrel with my own definition of Genius. I've got a hunch *Genius is just Horse Sense with Wings.* For a written explanation of this saying, write me at Cooga Mooga; enclose the top of an old Chevrolet with your request.

Now the big question is: how is an individual (you) to learn and earn this magic of heroes, soothsayers, and geniuses?

How to Develop Horse Sense:

Hoss sense comes hard. Without experience we're usually governed by what we want rather than what's good for us. That's why the parent's lot can be a tough one. Like when you were a little kid. Mamma tries to be logical with Junior and appeal to the horse sense he doesn't have yet. She says, "Look, li'l darlin', I'd love to buy you the cake and the ice cream and the candy, but if I do you'll get sick. Now do you want to listen to Mamma, or do you want to be sick?" And Junior comes right back with "I want to be sick!"

You see—no experience. Junior hasn't *been* sick yet. But once should be enough. The sages through the ages have warned us that "there's no substitute for experience"—and there isn't. Dad says, "Hortense, if you hang on that clothes line, it'll break and you'll fall." You do. It does. You do. So far, so good. You've gathered some experience. But now, horse sense should take over and two things should happen. You don't hang on the clothes line again (logic, or the law of cause and effect has been born in your thinking—"I do this—this follows") which means that you have "profited by the experience." Second, you begin to regard Dad in a new light. He's an expert who can prophesy from his own knowledge—and now you begin to "profit by the experience of others"—which will spare you a lot of personal, experimental lumps. Which is good, because sometimes lumps leave scars.

Some develop this horse sense more slowly than others and that's called "learning the hard way." And when it comes to ethical and moral values it can be disastrous to "learn the hard way." . . . like at Sing Sing! Here's a minor example. Suppose the third grade teacher told me that I must *memorize* the multiplication tables and such erratic spelling as *no, sew, bow,* and *hoe,* and I eventually fail long division and arrive in high school writing such masterly prose as, *"No,* don't *so* the *bo* on the *ho."* Or, *"New,* don't *sew* the *bew* on the *hew."* Or even, *"Noe,* don't *sow* the *bew* on the *ho."* Someone is apt to suspect I haven't got the sense of a flea, let alone a horse. And eventually, if repeated experiences fail to awaken our common sense, if we go from trouble with our parents, to trouble with our teachers, to trouble with the law, it's quite likely we'll qualify for the tart label Benjamin Franklin dropped (in the name of Poor Richard) when he said: "Experience keeps a hard school, but *fools* will learn in no other." How about that now?

So the seed of horse sense sprouts with experience, but it doesn't grow until you begin to profit by that experience and it won't branch out into a real hero-maker until you can also profit by the experience of others, and until *you can evaluate* what you learn and observe. For instance, if every time we had a fizzle, that first fall off a two-wheel bike, or the first time the left ski goes east, the right ski goes west, and we go south, we decided that this was a clothes-line that broke and we'd never do *that* again, well, pretty soon we'd be afraid to do much of anything.

But by applying Horse Sense we can tell when *not* to repeat an experiment and when to *try, try again.* We'll refuse to be *fools,* but we will also refuse to be failures.

Mark Twain, one of the great spinners of homespun philosophy remarked, "We should be careful to get out of an experience only the wisdom that is in it—and stop there; lest we be like the cat that sits down on a hot stove-lid. She will never sit down on a hot stove-lid again—and that is well; but also she will never sit down on a cold one anymore."

A few years back a gallant gal, Florence Chadwick, after successfully swimming the English channel, became the first woman to attempt to swim the twenty-one miles from Catalina Island to the California coast. Thousands of TV fans watched her battle all night through icy water, fog, and schools of sharks, only to be pulled from the water a mile short of her goal, exhausted, humiliated, chilled—in a word, defeated.

Now right there she could have decided that the Catalina channel was a hot stove-lid and she'd never sit on *that* one again. But Florence, in evaluating her two experiences, remembered that at the same point in her English swim when she felt she had gone as far as she could go, she begged to be taken from the water. And right then her father sighted land! "I saw it, too," she recalled, "and that gave me the push I needed to go on and make it. But in my unsuccessful attempt to cross the Catalina fog obscured the land ahead. When they told me it was only a mile away I didn't have the faith to believe what I couldn't see. I had lacked *faith,* not *ability.*"

When she evaluated these two experiences she decided, first, *that the objective was worthwhile;* and then that *with a better effort she could get a better result.* She had to try again. This was "good, plain, logical thinking founded on experience."

Two months later, with renewed faith, Florence Chadwick turned her defeat into victory, became the first woman to swim the Catalina channel despite recurring fog, and beat the men's record by two hours.

And that, my friend, generally speaking, is how Horse Sense makes Heroes. Now let's get specific.

Sense and Nonsense:

One of the most important things you can know is—what you don't know. And one of the most sensible things you can do is—admit it!

Once you've taken the plunge it's a lot easier than ad-libbing. Turning again to our Horse Sense philosophers for confirmation we find Mark Twain saying: "I was gratified to be able to answer promptly and I did. I said that I didn't know."

Kids who have to give an answer for everything, right or wrong, who can't bear to confess that there is an area not covered by their personal knowledge and experience are all-show-and-no-go, believe me! They can also be dangerous as a source of much misinformation—and that's being polite about the whole thing. Josh Billings in his Farmer's Allminax allowed: "It is better to know nothing than to know what ain't so."

Actually, you should guard against *giving* misinformation as well as *receiving* it, because a lie is a lie, regardless of the fancy name you give it—and has a way of spreading like the ripples on a pond where a pebble is dropped, until more and more people "believe what ain't so." In Horse Sense lingo it goes like this: "One of the most striking differences between a cat and a lie is that a cat has only nine lives."—while nonsense doubles itself indefinitely every time it is spoken into another pair of ears.

I remember once when there was some confusion about whether we were going to have school on Lincoln's birthday. One of the "know-it-all" guys told his girl we were, although he really didn't have any straight dope. And his girl told her best friend, who told her brother, who told his girl, who told —well—the next day, Lincoln's birthday, we all showed up moanin' and groanin' at school only to find the doors locked and the teachers snoozing away at home. In this case there was no real harm done, but when the same kind of misinformation spreads on more important subjects, marriage, or sex, or the laws of the land, or religion, the results can be pretty serious.

So, if you don't know, say so!

"Keep cool!" say the experts. "Use your head!"

Do you remember when Alice, in Wonderland, was talking to the Mad Hatter? "Really, now you ask me," said Alice, very much confused, "I don't think—" "Then you shouldn't talk," said the Hatter. And you shouldn't act either. James Thurber advised: "He who hesitates is sometimes saved." And American Horse Sense shouts: *"Before you louse it up —THIMK!"*

I remember a girl, a very bright, sweet, attractive gal, who became engaged to a buddy of mine in college. He was crazy about her—but she had him worried. "I hate to set the date," he told me one day, "because, well—she's just about perfect except that she panics out in a pinch." Her pattern was, in every crisis, whether her mother was ill or a new dress wasn't ready in time for a dance, to have hysterics or run away, and her husband-to-be wasn't sure she could be trusted with the responsibilities of married life. She'd get "too shook" under pressure. It was so serious with him that he tried talking to her about it, but she just shrugged and said: "That's just the way I am. I guess I was born that way."

But this isn't true. Finley Peter Dunne, a Chicago newspaperman, helped the cause of Horse Sense along by inventing an American philosopher with an Irish accent, named Mr. Dooley. Mr. Dooley used to talk over profound problems with his friend, Mr. Hennessy—and one of their discussions centered around this very subject.

"Oh, well," said Mr. Hennessy, "we are as th' Lord made us."

"No," said Mr. Dooley, "lave us be fair. Lave us take some of th' blame oursilves."

Nobody's "just born that way." It's the pattern they develop and it's always possible to change that pattern. My friend had quite a time convincing his girl that she could *consciously choose her reactions* until they became dependable and habitual. Finally she began to "get the message" that she wasn't going to be married until she got with it and then, as Wellington suggests, she was so "strongly intent on an object" that she was directed to the right method. She found that what she continually demanded of herself, she finally became. With his help she schooled herself to stop a moment and think, to handle fear and panic and indecision with a determination to be calm and intelligent, to "use her head" instead of her heels. Today they're married and she's that "best of all home remedies," a good wife and mother. She's all there in a pinch!

Mickey Mantle, one of the greatest hitters in baseball, had to do some pattern-changing, too. At fifteen Mickey played short-stop week-ends on the Spavinaw, Oklahoma, team while his dad pitched. Before long Mickey was playing professional ball in the minor leagues and finally he got his big chance with the New York Yankees. "I'd flash sometimes. More often I'd fizzle," Mickey says of those days. Then, in a double header in Boston he struck out five times in a row. "I cried like a baby," Mickey says, "blubbered to Manager Stengel, 'Put someone else in my place who can hit the ball.'" Stengel not only replaced him but shortly Mickey Mantle was back in the minor leagues. His dad came to Kansas City to meet him. Mickey told his dad, "I guess I don't have it as a Big Leaguer. I belong in the minors." And then his dad told Mickey: "Mickey, things get tough at times and you must learn to take it. If that's all the guts you've got you don't belong in baseball."

Mickey's dad left. Mickey stayed. He stuck until his reactions under pressure were consistent. He didn't blubber. He didn't fizzle. He worked until he was hitting again, and then he worked some more until he was back with the Yankees. And that's how Horse Sense helped make Mickey Mantle a champion!

If we begin as teen-agers (or even before), we can learn what it takes to meet the unexpected in a truly heroic fashion. We can handle big emergencies or small problems without being thrown off our stride. But we have to stick with it, insist on the common sense reaction until it becomes a habit. If you don't believe the Horse Sense of that, well, here it is again from the horse's mouth—Josh Billings, in the Farmer's Allminax: "Consider the postage stamp. Its usefulness consists in the ability to stick to one thing 'til it gets there."

Winged-Horse Sense:

Do you remember an old song called "You'd Be So Nice To Come Home To"? It began to appeal to my vocal chords when I first met Shirley—and since we've been married I've just changed the tense. She *is* so nice to come home to!

The point is that I got a new slant on that song from something Fannie Hurst, the famous novelist, said about her husband. In all the years she'd known him, she said, she couldn't remember him doing a thing she wished he hadn't done. "How come?" she asked him. "How can you be so consistently mindful of others?"

And he said, quite simply, "I suppose because *I have to live with myself.*"

So far we've discussed Horse Sense as applied to the outside world of people and events. But here, in one sentence, is Horse Sense with Wings—the casual statement of a man who had found the magic for *living with himself.* If we, too, can take this one further step we'll know what "that towering feeling" is all about because the height of "good, plain, logical thinking" leads us to the conclusion that, always and always, we're going to come home to *us.* We don't *have* to marry Bill or Edith and come home to them. We don't *have* to settle on the Sahara and come home to a tent, or squat inside the Arctic Circle and come home to an igloo. We can choose where we want to live, and with what partner. But we've *got* to live with ourselves, take ourselves with us wher-

ever we go, and after every party, after school, after a test
or a sports event we've got to come home and be alone with
ourselves. You want to make that a pleasant experience,
don't you? Well, whether it is or not will boil down to the
ethical values and moral standards *you* set for *you!*

This is true for presidents and milk men, old ladies and
young ladies, poor folk and rich folk. Miss Hurst tells of a
brush she once had with her good friend, the late Fiorello
LaGuardia, one of New York City's great mayors and a
man of high ideals, fiery temper, quick decisions and sometimes a quick tongue. Once, when the mayor had publicly
scolded one of his co-workers, Miss Hurst wrote her old
friend a questioning letter. She heard nothing from the
mayor until one day she received a large box containing yellow roses and a smaller tin box with a note which read: "Yellow roses and a box of pills, from Fiorello. I think your liver
must be out of order." But underneath he had written:
"Why did I do that to MacGregor? I haven't been able to
look at myself since. I love that man. I hate me." Miss Hurst
called this a "portrait of even a big man not wanting to go
home to himself."

Now in this light the first things we see if we are sensible
are the things that make us uncomfortable later—outbursts
of temper, the temptation to look at someone else's test or
homework, the desire to "chop" a friend to be smart, to be-
little someone in order to feel "big-shot" ourselves, or to do
something in a weak moment that we don't honestly believe is morally right. Why? Sure, it may hurt the other guy.
But if we're honest we'll be as big as the ex-Mayor and admit it hurt us more. When we come home to us, when we're
alone, we "hate us."

In the new Testament, Jesus, who knew all this and loved
us very much, gave us the very best rules for Horse Sense
with Wings. You can find them very easily and they help a
lot. He said, among other things, not only don't kill—but
don't be angry, or call people fools. Make friends with your

enemies. Forgive your brother. Give rather than grab. Treat others the way you want to be treated. This is the highest order of Horse Sense, not only to keep your dealings with others well greased, but because it is the *best* and *quickest* and most practical way for you to like you.

Jesus also said to *pray*.

It's hard to be brave, or heroic, or the kind of people we truly want to be without prayer. Benjamin Franklin said: "It is hard for an empty sack to stand up straight," and even after we've rid ourselves of the unwanted furnishings there is still the job of refilling and refurnishing, until we are content to live with ourselves and are ready for anything life can bring us.

Prayer is our point of contact with the Power that can actually refill and refurnish—and make us what we want to be!

That power is God, and God's power is not only very real, but always available, in every need, in every crisis, for guidance, for courage, for every good thing. God is "a very present help in trouble."

And because this is true, *you can prove it.*

Here's an example from the ol' Boone Scrap Book of a beautiful prayer obviously formed by someone who had discovered this truth. And it brought the necessary power for the highest courage to a young girl in a very great deal of trouble.

It was written by a teen-ager in the sixteenth century while she waited in the Tower of London for them to cut her head off. The gently reared English princess, Lady Jane Grey, talented, sensitive, devout, probably never even dreamed that at sixteen she would be faced with the unexpected—forced to marry against her wishes—made a helpless pawn in a game of king-making, with the throne of England as the prize —finally faced with public execution on Tower Hill shortly after her seventeeth birthday. But that's exactly what happened to her. For ten miserable days that sixteen-year-old girl sat unwillingly on a tipsy throne as Queen and when it toppled she found herself locked in the Tower condemned of High Treason. Lady Jane Grey met her death, unresisting and courageous at just about the age when I was worrying about what to wear to the senior banquet. If we'd changed places, would I have been an empty sack? Would you? Here is the prayer written by this teen-ager while she awaited her execution—the prayer I personally think must have filled her with the strength she urgently needed.

"O Merciful God, be Thou now unto me a strong tower of defence, I humbly entreat Thee. Give me grace to await Thy leisure, and patiently to bear what Thou doest unto me; nothing doubting or mistrusting Thy goodness towards me; for Thou knowest what is good for me better than I do. Therefore do with me in all things what Thou wilt; only arm me, I beseech Thee, with Thine armour, that I may stand fast; above all things, taking to me the shield of faith; praying always that I may refer myself wholly to Thy will, abiding Thy pleasure, and comforting myself in those troubles which it shall please Thee to send me, seeing such troubles are profitable for me; and I am assuredly persuaded that all Thou doest cannot but be well; and unto Thee be all honour and glory. Amen.—"

(Lady Jane Grey, 1537-1554)

3

Where Are the Pearls in Your Oyster?

"... Tinker, Tailor, Cowboy, Sailor,
Doctor, Lawyer, or Indian Chief ... ?"

How about it? Which one will you be? We've agreed that finding your personal talents and individual identity is one of the big teen-time challenges. You can't stall around too long. (And counting your buttons to the cadence of a nursery rhyme isn't really a scientific solution to the problem.)

The other night I heard a brilliant middle-aged business executive comment on your generation. "Most teen-agers," he said, "live by the old saw 'The World Is My Oyster'." (And he and I, and certainly you, old chum, know that is potentially true.) "But," he added, "the idea has gotten around these days that it's served up on the half-shell all ready to be devoured. It isn't. It has to be opened and that is a tricky proposition." And that's true, too!

So now we get around to the proposition of how to open oysters. Remember the oyster you have to open is your *own*

—and the process can be confusing. If you don't believe it, try to follow this gem:

A logician said he would prove an opened oyster to be better than heaven, and he attempted it by this curious argument.

"An opened oyster is better than nothing—and nothing is better than heaven. *Ergo* an opened oyster is better than heaven."

Now this gent has both his pearls and his marbles rattling, I think, but I assure you that finding the pearls in your oysters (or talents in your make-up) is a project in which heaven has a great interest. I think I'd put it this way: Jesus likened the "Kingdom of Heaven" to a pearl of great price and said it is "within" you. Part of this hidden treasure is the potential, or talent, God has given you.

So—what's the exact challenge? And what's the procedure to solve it?

The challenge is finding the particular door in this big, wide, wonderful world labeled "You."

Today, like most every other day, your mail bag philosopher pulled a batch of letters out of the bag and heaped 'em up on the desk at Cooga Mooga (my office). I hadn't opened many when I ran across one from a 'tween-gal named Kris.

"What, me worry?" she writes. "I haven't got a problem in the world worth a four cent stamp. I think being fifteen and a sophomore in high school is just about the most exciting age there is. There are so many things I can do and so many futures to choose from that I can't make up my mind!" I know how she feels. You investigate like mad, learning a little bit about a lot of things, trying to settle on the future that interests you most. Reading books—and books. And everything you read, I mean *everything* from comics to science fiction to Twisted Tales from Shakespeare by Richard Armour to *un*twisted plays *by* Shakespeare—everything you read just gives you a lot more mental traveling to do and cross-roads to decide on.

Kris isn't finished yet. "Really, Pat, the only problem I have is that I need at least forty-eight and a half hours in each day. What I'm writing about is this. I've read your book and your articles and I wondered if you ever had this problem? I mean, I've got to make up my mind pretty soon about what to do with my life. Right now, I'm just mixed up in a maze. Can you help? Please answer soon. Your friend, Kris."

A maze, in case you were never in one, is an endless and confusing series of passageways with many dead ends—but only one exit!

I get the message, doll. You're having fun but you're beginning to realize that you can't go prancing around investigating by-paths all your life. You're about due for some decisions (there we go again—decisions—decisions—*decisions*) as to which exact turns will bring you out most happily into the big world of your future.

Was I ever there? I was. I sho 'nuff was. And whether you call it a "maze" or "diving for pearls" or "opening oysters" (this gal mixed my metaphors on me!) I have a direct line open to you this very minute. And I'll say this—I'd like to send copies of this kind of letter (instead of my personal opinions) to answer the worried-type adults who write me now and then quacking and quaking over the future of the "younger generation." As long as most young folks are exploring and developing their talents their futures look safe and exciting to me!

I know that at fifteen I popped around like popcorn in a hot skillet or a guy trying to open an oyster with a cork screw. During the winter months I was determined to be the doctor who found a cure for the common cold. In the spring, when I wasn't dreaming of being tagged by the New York Yankees, I was planning to be an explorer and unearth King Solomon's mines. I even had a get-rich-quick scheme that involved stacks of comic books I'd saved which, in fifty years, I figgered would be collectors' items, although looking back I'm not so sure I'd call waiting fifty years a quick way to make a fortune. I was both a cartoonist and reporter on *The Pony Express,* our high school paper, and when I wasn't creating a world-stopping cartoon I was plotting ways to set the old planet in better motion with a by-lined column to be called: "Earth Is My Beat." We hadn't gotten around to the Moon then.

In the summer I was an apprentice carpenter at seventy-five cents an hour with the Boone Construction Company, and if you're thinking the similarity in names got me the job, you're right. But Dad's partiality ended right there and my brother Nick and I kept those jobs by trying to work twice as hard as any of Dad's other employees, even though the building business, for me, was a dead dead-end almost from the beginning.

At fifteen I was also a "semi-professional" singer, professional when the Kiwanis Club or the Lions paid me five dollars to sing pop and Western numbers at their banquets and semi when the Shakespeare Club (to eat or not to eat—that was the question) paid me with a free meal for doing the same thing. I was also entering every possible type singing contest and it was like being addicted to revolving doors because I always came out just where I went in—no where! Since I was breaking all records for losing contests, when I thought of choosing a college it was with the idea of teaching (English or Speech preferred) or getting into educational TV. I, too, was dashing up one dead end after another, having a wonderful time investigating; and then suddenly, after losing all those contests in Nashville, Tennessee, I found myself on a straight, straight path that led me into the big, big world via Ted Mack's Amateur Hour and the Arthur Godfrey Talent Scouts in New York, and a hit Dot recording, *Two Hearts, Two Kisses,* in Chicago. I popped out of my "maze" a singer—loving every minute of it.

The point is that few of us know, in the early teens, just where or when or how we'll emerge. But on that *where* and *when* and *how* hangs the fate of the world. Big talk? You bet. You have to use big talk to put over big ideas. And here is a big, *big,* BIG one.

The World of Tomorrow already belongs to those of you searching your way through that teen-age maze today.

Out of it will come our future presidents, our first ladies, the doctor who will lick cancer, our statesmen with blueprints for peace, the mothers who will raise another Young America, the teachers who will teach it, space men and women and maybe the first couple to pioneer living on Mars. What else? You name it! Whatever *you* can conceive and execute will be part of that World of Tomorrow.

Yesterday, when I was kicking around somewhere 'twixt twelve and twenty, I was just as excited as Kris and you. I, too, was befuddled by all the possible choices. But I found that I was also a little puzzled because I couldn't help noticing some strange, sad things. First I found that a lot of college students, and even so-called grown-ups, were still buzzing around in the maze, up one blind alley after another. Haphazardly they were flitting from place to place, ambition to ambition, crashing their heads and cursing their luck.

And then there was another group, lots of them with long adult faces, some of them with long gray beards. This is the group that stopped years before right inside the front entrance, not even attempting to get through the maze, found themselves a neat little rut and dug in. There they sat, complaining bitterly that opportunity had passed *them* by.

Well, maybe. But to me, looking back now, that maze is no maze at all really, but an exciting, very special teen-age land where every twist and turn presents a challenge and an opportunity. It's a God-given testing time and we're supposed to make the most of it. There's some magic in it, too, 'cause each one of the interests you have is a key which may unlock for you a door that would be a dead-end to me forever. Each of us, according to our individual talents, has a path through the maze that is exclusively our own, that, if we persist until we find it, brings us out into the world as happy, successful, useful and unique human beings, remember?

Now, how can *you* best find *your* particular way?

Direction Finders:

To guide you through the maze of opportunities to that door marked "You"—it just happens that we all have a "Compass" built in from birth—if we'll just use it. It has 6 parts that have to be oiled and set in motion if we're not to get bogged down or confused.

First, there's *Imagination*. You have to dream! That might raise a few adult eyebrows, because I know parents and teachers who "allow as how" whenever a teen-ager is assigned a chore or a good stiff piece of homework he's off immediately in a cloud of day dreams. They're not talking about you, are they? Well, anyway, this is the wrong kind of imagination for the purposes I have in mind.

Here's the idea.

One afternoon, when I was out in Hollywood making *Journey To The Center Of The Earth,* I grabbed a couple of spare hours for a trek to the Los Angeles Public Library. I like grazing through libraries and I browsed eventually into the Social Science room. A flock of High School seniors appeared to have strayed in ahead of me. They were huddled in one part of the room, buzzing like bees. I couldn't resist asking the librarian what had caused this astoundin' migration.

"Oh, they're doing a term paper on Vocations," she informed me in a strenuous library whisper. "Every year about now we're mobbed when some of the English teachers hand out this assignment."

"They certainly seem to know what they want," I whispered back.

She laughed. "There is information on over four hundred vocations catalogued in separate folders in that enormous filing cabinet over there—everything from Accounting to

Zoology—and each year nine-tenths of them fight over *six* folders. The boys want *Lawyer, Doctor,* and *Engineer,* in that order, and the girls *Air Line Hostess, Model,* and *Nurse.*

Now that's an example of limited imagination that could unbalance the world as completely as an H-bomb. Think of it! Stewardesses with no pilots to fly them. Models with no designers or textile manufacturers to put the clothes on their backs. Doctors with no druggists. Nurses with no hospitals. Engineers with no concrete. Lawyers with no Peter Gunns to catch them clients. No TV. No singers. No department stores. No farms. Like help!

My curiosity over those three hundred ninety-four spurned vocations wouldn't stop until I had a look at the files. The seniors had overlooked some goodies, too—like *Puppetry.* If they were the kind of eight year olds that I was, to make a living at Puppetry would be almost as much of a lark as singing. And for something different—well, did you know that the *Blacksmith* is not extinct? In fact, a man that's handy with a hammer and anvil today could command $3.00 an hour. Then there were such novelties as *Rigging,* and *Scrap,* and *Catering,* and fat folders on old faithfuls like *Teaching, Social Service, Newspapers.*

The outlook for women has widened and widened since the days of the bustle and side-saddle—even since the days of the Bloomer Girl—until practically the only spot that hasn't been graced by a fair female is that of the chief executive.

And did you know that a woman was nominated for president over three-quarters of a century ago? 'S truth! Mrs. Belva A. Lockwood was the candidate of the Equal Rights Party in 1884.

But you girls can still be as limited as you were in the side-saddle days if your vision doesn't travel beyond Air Line Hostess, Model, or Nurse. Also, I have a horrible feeling that some of those tired guys I saw sitting around the entrance to the maze swearing opportunity had passed them by were the very ones that couldn't dream anything besides Lawyer, Doctor, Engineer, and who found those fields out of reach either time-wise, money-wise, or talent-wise.

It seems to me that the people who get in a rut, who come out of high school or college without a direction, settle disinterestedly for the first job they can get and then plow it for the rest of their lives, bog down because that Imagination needle isn't swinging freely.

If yours is rusty or stiff you can loosen it by reading about people who do all kinds of things, by talking to policemen, janitors, teachers, and seeing how they like their jobs. By pursuing hobbies. By increasing your curiosity, your observation, your sense of wonder. By watching for occupations on TV and portrayed in movies and then identifying yourself with them in—imagination.

The second needle that has to be set on your compass would seem to swing toward an opposite pole, but you need it for balance. It's *Realism.* You can call it being practical, down-to-earth, or whatever appeals to you, as long as you get it in motion. But if we don't couple this with our Dreams we'll be "kooks" with our heads in the clouds and no legs to move around on, or we'll be the long-faced gray beards who beat their heads on the stone walls of the maze all their days weeping over their "bad luck."

There's no realism in planning to be an opera singer and fill the Metropolitan with sound if you have a voice the size of mine, nor being a melody writer if you're tone deaf. Or a songwriter if you believe as one girl did, that "a lyric is something written to be sung by a liar." And how about me being a collector of comic books when I knew full well Mamma would give the whole bunch to the first Boy Scout who rang the bell for a paper drive? (Which she did!) My math was too limited for engineering. From a practical viewpoint, by the time I could have gotten my M.D. and gone to work on the common cold, my wife and kiddies would have starved. As for the New York Yankees, it looks like Mickey Mantle still has a good year or two left in him.

After shopping in town the other day the lovely Mrs. B came up with an illustration for our reality chat. In a dress shop Shirley was waited on by a very enthusiastic, very young lady who decided to confide in her (Shirley affects people like that). The girl just loved pretty clothes, she said. She loved the dress shop. She had always dreamed of working in a place like this. But when she brought out a dress for Shirley to try on, she remarked, "Now here's a little number that will never go out of style. It'll just go on looking ridiculous year after year."

I complimented her sense of humor. "But—realistically speaking," laughed my wife, "she should either get more training or get into some other branch of the business. She lacks the natural sales touch."

A buddy of mine who teaches in high school told me that since the science fiction craze has been coupled with the big push Moonward, many of his freshman students dream of being scientists. "And some of them will make it," he said. "But for quite a number it just isn't practical. Take the young dreamer who committed this amazing idea to paper: "To separate hydrogen from oxygen in water (H_2O), evaporate the wet part and the rest is oxygen." Very little talent for being exact in an exact field, huh? Or would you have said the same thing? Don't look at me—I don't know how, either!

You get the idea? Unless we check our dreams against our true potential and all the facts available, things just get mazier and mazier (I'm not sure there's such a word but it says what I mean, anyway).

To get your Reality needle swinging freely it's a good idea to work as an apprentice when and where you can. Try sizing yourself up honestly and then discuss your aptitude for the things that appeal to you with impersonal observers like teachers or personal ones like parents, who often know things about our character and potential that we don't know ourselves. Read practical books as well as the kind that stimulate the imagination. *Go to the library and browse.* There's nothing square about a library (except the shape of the rooms). Honest!

In the Social Science section, a good starting point, you can get The Occupational Outlook Handbook, a fascinating master guide put out and kept up to date by the United States Department of Labor. It not only lists most known vocations but describes each one briefly and clearly tells the Nature of the Work, Necessary Training, and Other Qualifications, Employment Outlook (your chances of getting a job), Earnings, Working Conditions, and Where To Go For More Information. Now that's what I call practical, chum!

Equally fascinatin' and realistic are the number of "supporting roles" required to keep each major industry, profession, and what have you, in full operation. Most of us start with dreams of being *the Star* in a given field. If medicine attracts you, naturally you first want to be a doctor or nurse. But if everyone is to star, who'll do the technical and lab work? Who'll fill the prescriptions? Who'll plan the hospital meals for the patients? Or you like the smell of grease paint and the world of entertainment? So, of course, you want to be an actor or an actress, a singer or a dancer. But what if you can't act? Or sing? Or dance? Does that mean that to be realistic you have to give up this world of glamor? Not if you can sew. Or handle electricity. Or man a camera. No production ever went on without the full cooperation of the wardrobe mistress. No TV stage was ever visible without the electrician. No movie was ever "put in the can" without the cameramen. Don't think there isn't real satisfaction in these jobs, either.

Robert Henri, a well-known artist, told about the time he attended a private showing in a famed New York art gallery. He was admiring a fine canvas by Sargent when his attention was distracted by a big, brawny fellow standing beside him who looked like anything but a painter. "They have given me a good place at last," the fellow muttered to himself.

Henri couldn't resist asking, "Are you in this line of work?"

The man nodded. "Been in it twenty years and this is the first time I ever got such a good showing."

"Indeed?" Henri was puzzled. "And which is your work?"

"Right there," the man indicated the canvas in front of which they both stood, with satisfaction.

"That . . . why, Sargent painted that," Henri said.

"Painted it? Oh, yes. I think Sargent was the name of the fellow who painted the picture. But it was me that made the frame."

He and Sargent *were* in the same line of work and he was proud of it.

Now, to keep us pliable while **Dreams** and **Realism** pull us first one way and then another, there's another important compass point—*Flexibility.* Flexibility is, so far as I can see, a mixture of fifty per cent Courage and fifty per cent Humor. You have to be daring enough to try things and able to laugh at yourself if you fall on your face.

So you want to be a ballet dancer? You study hard, stretch, bend, practice faithfully for years. And you can't make the grade. Are you going to fall apart? What if you've devoted your college years to a specialty, gotten your degree, and then find that you've no real taste for that profession? Are you gonna sit down inside the maze and sulk? Or are you equipped to start again? I've always been fascinated by the ability of people who have humor and courage to bounce right back and take another tack.

Robert Casey, for instance, the famous newspaperman, after getting a college degree, was forced by economic necessity (he was broke) to take a job as bookkeeper in a sawmill. He found it was contrary to his talents (he never could balance the books), and his taste (he hated figures). So what did he do? He resurrected an old dream and betook himself to a newspaper office.

"What makes you think you could be a reporter?" the city editor asked.

"Because," said the practical Casey, "I don't know anything about bookkeeping."

"Do you feel that being a reporter is what you want most in the world?" he was asked.

"I want to be a chemical engineer," confessed Casey, "but I've only got one lung."

"One lung is enough," said the city editor. "But, if you haven't patience enough to keep books you wouldn't do well with chemistry."

"I didn't say anything about patience," Casey said.

"You don't have to," the editor said. "You haven't got any. I'll put you on. Next Saturday you'll either get $18.00 for the week or you'll get fired."

Casey may not have had patience but he had courage and humor. He was flexible. So was one Jim Mulroy who came to a Chicago paper straight from a steam laundry—and won a Pulitzer Prize. And another guy who did very well in the United Press to which he had delivered milk for several years.

Add to Dreams, Realism, Flexibility, three more direction finders and we should be able to find and stay on the beam. The additions are: *Enthusiasm, The Ability to Work,* and a *Purpose*.

Enthusiasm is what makes one girl consider baby sitting a way to "meet interesting people" and another feel it is just a well-paid chore. It's a fresh point of view that cuts right through old established methods (say the horse and buggy) and comes up with something new (say a car or a plane). What if Henry Chevrolet hadn't had enthusiasm?

It was enthusiasm that raised a very young lieutenant in the Russia of the czars to the rank of Captain in a single day. When the lieutenant took charge of the guard at the St. Petersburg Winter Palace he noted an empty white bench on the beautiful expanse of lawn. He noted further that two guards flanked the bench round the clock. Each set was relieved every three hours. Nobody knew why. But enthusiasm for his first command prodded the young lieutenant to some detective work. He found an old man who had once been in charge of the palace archives. The old man remembered this story: "During the reign of Peter the Great, two hundred years ago," he said, "that bench got a new coat of paint. The czar was afraid the ladies might get wet paint on their dresses so he ordered a guard to watch the bench. The order was never rescinded. Then in 1908 all the palace guards were doubled for fear of revolution—so the bench has had two guards ever since." The situation was corrected and the lieutenant became a captain the next day.

Enthusiasm is an eye opener and this lieutenant may well have been the Russian Corporal Presley of his day.

Now, when we come to talk about *Purpose* we're really discussing the wheel on which our whole compass spins. What is our motive? Why enter the maze at all? Why not sit under a cork tree like Ferdinand the Bull and smell the flowers? If our *primary* purpose is to make money, to "be a big wheel," we might just as well ask ol' Ferdinand to move over now.

Do you remember the go-getter who saw an Indian chief squatting silently at the door of his tepee somewhere out west and went up to him and asked: "Chief, why don't you get yourself a job?"

"Why?" grunted the chief.

"Well, you could earn a lot of money."

"Why?" said the chief.

"Oh, if you worked real hard and saved your money, you'd soon have a big bank account. Wouldn't you like that?"

"Why?" asked the chief.

"Well," shouted the go-getter, "with a big bank account

you could retire and then you wouldn't have to work any more."

"Not working now," said the chief.

No, "to earn a lot of money" isn't a good enough "Purpose." On the other hand, to believe that it isn't cricket to have wall-to-wall carpet, a jazzy car, maybe even a back yard swimmin' hole, if you can earn them, is to be too unrealistic. According to the Bible, the workman is always worthy of his hire. In other words, it's okay to enjoy your earnin's.

That great legal mind, Clarence Darrow, found a subtle way of impressing this on some club women in a mid-western city. He had given a lecture on Phoenician Art, Customs, and Culture. After the applause died down the club president rose, fluttered, and said, "Mr. Darrow, I don't know *how* we can thank you." With the commanding presence that made him famous in the courtroom, Mr. Darrow immediately returned to the platform and said: "I forgot to tell you that it was the Phoenicians who first invented Money." So money is to get neither too much nor too little emphasis. It has its place.

What purpose, then, besides money, should spur us on in our search for a life's work? It seems to me that our natural aim should be two-fold—*Creativity and Service*. In a book called *Charting Your Course* (Macrae Smith Company, Philadelphia) which I found while browsing in the library (Social Science room), the author, Henry S. Galus, speaking specifically to teen-agers; broke the opportunities for creativity and service into thirteen major fields. He said you could work *to feed people, to shelter them, supply their daily needs, service those daily needs, to protect people, transport them, inform them, entertain them, to heal, help, improve their spiritual life, their material life, and to serve all the people.* To me this is a terrific approach. You can turn these round and make them into questions.

Is *informing people* the thing I most want to do? If so,

what are my choices? I can be a teacher, a newspaperman, a writer, a radio commentator, to name only a few. Do I wish to *entertain* them? Yes! Well, I, P. Boone, will sing out and hope for the best. But you might wish to write music, or TV scripts. Or learn stage make-up. You see how it goes. Each major field encompasses many allied vocations.

Now I have a personal addition to make to this very fine list. Do you want to do the only thing that combines every one of these thirteen major fields—and is open only to a special segment of Young America? There is one vocation that offers this remarkable opportunity. It's *Homemaking. And the special segment includes every one of you girls.* (Sorry, fellas, you can skip the next two paragraphs. I'm left out, too.)

Girls, check the above list. Doesn't a wife-mother shelter, feed, inform, transport (oh, don't they transport!), entertain, heal, help, and so on? Perhaps this is why I've got such a special respect for homemakers. I'll admit we guys help a little with the shelter, food, protection, discipline, etc., but primarily the talent here belongs to you ladies. In this vocation no special training is ever wasted. So you have a good voice but not good enough for Broadway? I can promise you a more appreciative audience when you do your lullabies for the Sleeper Set at bedtime. You're a born comedian but not quite good enough for Hollywood? I'd love to sit at your dinner table. You're an ace at math but will settle for home and family instead of teaching? I wish you'd been in my family when I hit Algebra and Geometry. You studied bookkeeping? You'll get flowers from your husband when Income Tax time rolls 'round. You want to work for *all* the people? Perhaps you can raise a son worthy to be president of the United States. One of the greatest presidents we ever had, Abraham Lincoln, gave full credit for "all that I am or ever hope to be" to his mother. Certainly you can, under God, raise all your children to be good Americans.

Believe me, I have watched my own mother, my wife, the fine homemakers I know, and I can tell you that I truly think this is the most important objective any of my daughters could have in order to be fully creative and useful.

Did you ever think that in creativity and service man is really superior to anything else on this planet? It gives him true "dominion." A beaver can build a first class dam because that's what beavers *do*. It's race instinct. And a spider can spin a fine web. But the beaver can't suddenly decide to spin the web while the spider builds the dam. Nor can either of them carry laughter to a sick friend, water a thirsty flower, bind up the wounds of an antelope, or paint a picture that will bring more joy to the forest.

You see? It seems to me to be a divine trust to at least try to find and develop all the talents we possess, and to use them creatively in the service of other folks. Which throws me squarely up against a line that crops up in your letters from time to time: "I don't know if I have any talent but . . ." There are no *"buts." You have talent.* And I can prove it!

You and Your Talent:

I don't believe that there is such a thing in this world as a "no-talent" guy—or gal. I, personally, have never met one. I'll confess I don't know as many of you face-to-face as I wish I did, but I do get around quite a bit. I've met guys and gals who thought they could sing and couldn't. Or thought they could build a better mouse trap and didn't. But that only meant they were still in the maze. Later most of them found their right place and showed their true ability.

Y' know, sometimes I read over what I've written to you and get to thinking that maybe I'm trying to sound like an authority. Well, I've got news. I'm not. I'm just a slightly older guy sharing my experience with you because you've been nice to me, and I'd love to give you any boost I can. But when it comes to big things, I promised to play fair with you and back up my experience with real authority.

Now hear this—this is real authority!

Jesus, Himself, told a great story about this matter of talents, these pearls within us. He said "the kingdom of Heaven" was like a man who was going away on a long trip who gave gifts to his servants before he left. *He gave them talents.* (In those days, a talent was money.) He didn't give them all the same number; some got five, some two, some only one, but *everybody got something.* Then he went on his journey and when, after a long time, he returned, he asked them what they had done with his gifts. Now one of them had been afraid, and buried his talent, and the great man was anything but pleased. This servant got into a lot of trouble and was pretty unhappy. But to each one who had used his talents and accomplished something, the man said: *"Well done, thou good and faithful servant; thou hast been faithful over a few things, I will make thee ruler over many things; enter thou into the joy of thy lord."*

Isn't that a terrific promise? To find and use our talents, to increase them, is to enter into *joy.* That makes it a purpose with a purpose, right?

An expert named Trench in a famous lecture on "The Study of Words" referred to the use of the word "talents" in this parable recorded by St. Matthew. Copied here from that old Boone scrap-book, is what Trench said: "Men may choose to forget the ends for which their 'talents' were given them . . . they may practically deny that they were given at all; yet in this word . . . abides a continual memento that they were so given . . . and that each man shall have to render an account of their use."

But why forget or deny when the use of your talents means "joy"?

And so, happy maze to you, Kris—and Carl, and Joan, and Tom, and Sue, and all the thousands of you who have asked me in one way or another about your personal Talent Search. Remember, the search leads toward *joy.* The *pearl* in your own private oyster is the happy, successful, useful and fulfilled—YOU. I'm cheering for each and every one of you. Let me know how and where and when you come out!

4

Person-to-Person

I happened to see a composition, junior grade, the other day that left me gasping.

It was on geese: "Geese is a low, heavy-set bird which is mostly meat and feathers. Geese can't sing much on account of the dampness of the moisture. He ain't got not between-the-toes and he's got a little balloon in his stummick to keep from sinking. Some geese when they get big has curls on their tails and is called ganders. Ganders don't haff to sit and hatch but just eat and loaf and go swimming. If I was a goose, I'd rather be a gander."

Do you recognize that "If I was a goose, I'd rather be a gander" feeling? It has nothing to do with reversing the sexes, but do you ever start out the day feeling like Sir Walter Raleigh and wind up acting like Li'l Abner? Or go to a party all dressed up like a crown princess and suddenly, half way through the evening, wish you were a bare-foot Polynesian beach girl? You're just not what's called "socially secure," that's all. Not being "socially secure" is simply another part of being a teen-ager, because one of the big jumps to be made during that metamorphosis (or change) is from the law of the jungle that rules in the play-pen ("If you take my lollipop I'll whack you with your own fire engine") to the law of good fellowship—("Would you like half my lollipop?") and it's a big jump.

Most folks like you are eager for the transition. How do I know? Because the question that repeats itself most often in my mail bag, one way or another, is:

"How Can I Get Along Better with Other People?"

And I'll tell you right now that whether you're asking, "How can I make boys like me?", "Why don't the other girls accept me?", "Why doesn't my mother trust me?", or, "What does my teacher have against me?", it's the same basic question and a very important one. One we'll do our durndest to answer, too. It boils down to this—if you got along better with people, you'd be happy just being *you*, and not a goose *or* a gander!

It may make you feel a little better if I admit that I struggled with it myself.

More than once I've told the story of how my first "steady" romance broke up. It was during Christmas holidays of my freshman year. Jeanne and I had both tired of the goin' steady bit (after a quick three months), but neither of us could figure out how to let the other know. In the meantime, another gal, Kay, had caught my eye, and I wanted to be free to court her! Both gals went home for the holidays—so there I was.

Well, I came up with the perfect solution! I'd send Jeanne an inexpensive gift and a funny card; but Kay, out of the blue, would receive a very nice present and a note that would really set the stage for the new romance when school started again. I bought them each a compact; a dollar one for Jeanne, and a fancy eight-dollar beauty for Kay! (This blew my whole Christmas allowance.) Then I wrote the appropriate cards, wrapped the packages and sent them off. What a genius I was!

The only trouble was—I'd mixed up the addresses! Kay got the cheap gift and note intended for Jeanne and figured I was a stupid tightwad who couldn't even remember my own girl's name. And Jeanne—oh brother!—opened the expensive present which contained the sweet note to Kay! That did it. My goose was cooked and I was wishing *I'd* been a gander! Neither girl had much use for me after that.

I'm still trying to improve and a lot of people here in the adult world haven't got the hang of it *yet*. You don't have to be under twenty to need to know how to win friends—but if you learn it then you'll have a head start.

And the great thing is that there *are* laws of attraction— that they're the same for adults as for teen-agers—that *you* can learn them and be as likable and liked as you're willing to be. And I *do* mean *you!*

No Specialists Allowed:

First let's admit that if you are properly attractive you'll be popular with both sexes and all ages.

A truly attractive person is all-round attractive!

If you don't believe me now, you will when you see how the very same techniques—based on honest attraction—will land you a date, a best friend, help you get along with your parents, and make all your teachers perfectly bearable. (I should know. One of my best friends held over from my high school days was our principal, Mac Craig. He was, and still is, a very close friend. It can happen!)

So make up your mind that if you're specializing, you're missing something somewhere.

The People-Changing Business:

Second, if you aren't completely satisfied with any branch in your human relations department you'll have to be ready to make some changes—in you!

This is tough. 'Cause it often seems that, "If Susy Q. wasn't so high hat" or "Joe would stop telling lies about me" or "My mother was like *other* mothers" or "My Algebra teacher would say what she means" our little world would promptly settle into a nice groove. And maybe it would. But if you're realistic you'll admit sooner or later that changing other people is a long, difficult, even impossible task for the average teen-ager. And it really isn't necessary.

Granted, a lot of folks you meet could stand improvement. But try a "new" attitude on *your* part and see how "other people" change! It's humiliatin'! But rewardin'! So remember, teen-agers have no place in the People-Changing business on a broad scale. Your People-Changing, if you sho-nuff want to be liked, better be narrowed down to one person—you. And what changes for the better in the outer world is people's reaction to the New You.

Or Would You Rather Be a ————?

Third, the most attractive people in the world are the ones who are interested in others—turned outward in cheerfulness, kindness, appreciation, instead of turned inward to be constantly centered on themselves.

In childhood we've had pretty much everything handed to us on a silver tea tray without being called on to give too much in return. We're like the little boy who marched purposefully into a toy shop with a penny clutched tightly in his hand and drove the proprietor wild asking to see everything without making up his mind.

"Look here," said the proprietor finally, "what do you want for a penny—the whole world with a fence around it?"

Without hesitation the boy replied: "Let's see it."

But we're in for a rude awakening if we carry this "small world" idea from childhood to the next rung of the ladder. In the teen-age world we have to learn to give as well as get and friendship, we find, is a two-way-exchange-type proposition.

And if you'd rather get along better with people—well, how're you treating 'em?

Because the teen-age is a busy time (in that respect I'm still a teen-ager), a time of many adjustments and discoveries, it's also the natural time to fall into the trap of being completely wrapped up in our little selves, our little world, and to shrug off everything that doesn't affect us directly.

We're apt to notice very little of what's going on in any other play-pen—the adult one, for example.

Like I say, I never knew until our recent fishing trip what a rascal my own Granddaddy Pritchard had been! Now I see him in such a different, more human light. Mama and Daddy, over the years, have let us take a peek into *their* past when they thought it would help—and it did. It helped my brother and sisters and me; and I honestly think it helped Mama and Daddy, to feel that we all knew each other better.

If you want to "get along better with other people," the first check point is your own over-all attitude or personality. Ask yourself honestly: "Am I smiling, happy, friendly looking, at least as much interested in others as I am in me?" If you can say yay, you have an attracting attitude, a magnetic hook already out—a people-catcher. If not, here is the place to *start* building a New You.

What You Say and How You Say It:

Besides the first impact of your attitude or personality, which states your own estimate of yourself and what you want to be by a strong over-all impression which says: "I'm a lady"—"I'm a tramp"—"I'm fierce and bite strangers"—"I'm a nudnick"—"I'm a Harvard Man"—there are other speakers hooked up to the inside of you that make music if they're all working and in sync, or static if they're functioning badly . . .

Sometimes you think you're creating one impression on others when you really aren't, and sometimes you're creating an impression, possibly an unfavorable one, when you aren't aware of it. For instance, your *letters* tell me a lot about you. I know whether you're the thoughtful or the impulsive type, whether you're studious or social or a combination. I'd be able to identify Kris, who was in a "maze," in a crowded room! I can tell sometimes whether your room at home looks like a room in Buckingham Palace or a cyclone-cellar—all of this from what you write and how you write it. Have you ever noticed how much a thank-you note tells you about people? It's easy to spot a let's-get-this-chore-done frame of mind. Only occasionally you get one in which you detect a real note of gratitude and sincerity that makes you feel real appreciation.

That's communication by writing.

But telephone calls certainly come in on the vocal Public Relations wave band—and knowing when and how to use the telephone is a tune even some grown-ups can't play!

Now, it can be a big asset to teen-agers in getting along with others if they remember a few simple rules. Here they are: Get organized. Know what you want to say. Say it. Say good-bye.

It's a handy instrument—this telephone—for friendships, emergencies, conveniences. It can be an asset to teen-agers who find it hard to communicate with each other. If it's hard to say something face-to-face, it may be easier to try it on the phone—easier to create a good impression and break the ice. *But—the telephone should be a bridge—not a crutch*—to face-to-face communication.

And there seems to be one great telephone problem for teen-agers—when and how to get off. It can be a real embarrassment. You're through talking, neither of you knows how to say good-bye—or maybe you drop a hint or two and it doesn't work. If a girl's really gabby on the phone she can dampen a guy's spirits, and fast! Take a tip from one who knows and let him go, lover. I've seen cases where a guy went steady with a girl and the girl couldn't bear to let him get off the phone. In cases like this she really cools the whole thing off. The telephone technique is to say what you have to say, then hang up. Honest!

Both telephone and written communication take a back seat, though, to the *spoken word*. And while we've already discussed making your voice attractive—(trying to avoid sounding "like the shriek of a wild Yellow Cab calling to it's mate!") there's also the trick of saying attractive, friendly things in a courteous way *with* that voice.

Behind the instrument is the mind and heart that controls the words. You know the old ones about what you catch with vinegar and honey—and about what a soft answer will do. But what of the young man who was trying to get along better with a stand-offish gal—

"The day of great men has gone forever," she said.

"But the day of beautiful women has not," he said.

She bridled, smiled, wriggled in the honey and said, "I was only joking."

Or, the little boy who came home from a birthday party and his mother, checking on his manners, asked, "Are you sure you didn't ask Mrs. Jones for another piece of cake?"

"Oh, no, Mother, I only asked her for the recipe so you could make a cake like it, and she gave me two more pieces!"

Now that's using the old vocal chords to advantage in People-Catching!

One thing we have to resist, if we want to get along with folks, is the temptation to gossip, to tear our fellows down, to make ourselves look bigger at someone elses' expense, the "always belittlin' kids." I don't know what it is about us that makes us hate to see anybody a little better off or more talented than we are. This is guaranteed to drive folks away from you in droves. An anonymous gentleman versified it neatly:

> I hate those guys
> Who criticize
> And minimize
> Vigorous guys
> Whose enterprise
> Has helped them rise
> Above the guys
> Who criticize.

And if you find you're over-shy, or over-bold in conversation (a lion or a mouse—strangely these extremes both come from a common cause, too much self-*consciousness* plus too little self-*confidence*) here's a simple suggestion for getting the mind off the self and concentrated on the other fellow which will make talking easier and also fulfill the conditions for starting to build a new and more popular you! Jean Racine, the great French playwright, confided the secret of his personal popularity to his son thus: "Do not think I am sought after by the great because of my dramas . . . My talent with them (the great) consists not in making them feel that *I* have any talent but in showing them that *they* have."

Try, instead of building yourself up or worrying about the impression you're making, to make the other guy or gal feel happy, talented, important, and you'll forget your need to toot your own trumpet too loudly (it doesn't do any good, anyway)—or your fear of blowing it at all.

What You Do and How You Do It:

You remember that if you should elect to be a "gander," all you'd expect to do would be—"just to eat and loaf and go swimming." But even then, maybe you'd let Miss Goose in the water ahead of you, hmm? This would, I presume, be "gander manners."

And the things *you* do to be socially secure, what you decide to do and how you do it in the social sense come under the heading of manners. Your "manners" are how you perform the smaller segments of daily living—maybe no chance to be a hero here but if they're "good"—pleasant, easy, considerate—your social contacts will usually be "good"—pleasant and easy. If they are "bad," your contacts with others are sure to suffer.

There are, first of all, public manners—such as shopping, driving a car, taking your pets on the street and into public places. Shopping is one thing I'd like to avoid at all costs, even with my ever-lovin'. When we're about to enter a busy store I always think of the two sardines who were swimming about in New York harbor when one of them suggested that they go up to the Bronx for the week-end. "I'd rather not," objected the other, "it's too long a swim." "Then how about going by subway?" "What! . . . and be packed in like people!"

You gals don't know what you do to a guy in a store—but I've often wished that even the loveliest lady could *see* herself pawing over a bargain counter or *hear* herself talking to a sales girl. An awful lot of you check your manners at the door. It makes me think of a nice quiet man who went to a department store sale to pick up an item for his wife. He got in there but found two hundred women ahead of him. He stood around on one leg and the other for a while and wasn't getting anywhere fast. The goods were fading and he could see a disappointed wife in his mind's eye when he went home that night. Finally, at the end of a couple of hours, he discarded his cane and dignity and waded into the crowd. He stepped on an angry lady's foot and she said, "What's the matter with you? Can't you act like a gentleman?" He said, "Well, I've been acting like a gentleman for two hours and now I'm going to act like a lady."

It seems to me that, for the good of us all, we should change that economic law of supply and demand to a nicer social law of supply and *request*.

And here's a true and horrifying story of a young girl, aged thirteen, who was accused of shop-lifting. She was innocent, and her parents were indignant, but her behavior had certainly aroused suspicion as she and two friends flitted from counter to counter, picking up articles and dropping them in the wrong place, causing havoc instead of making their purchase and leaving. How about that?

As for driving, there are not only driving *laws,* but driving *manners.* It seems to me sometimes as if normally nice, well-

1. I don't usually get all dressed up to read a piece of music but this outfit is especially to say "Hi there!"

2. This is the first time I've seen you, Cherry, without my white bucks.

3. Even if you look very very closely the only male you'll find here is me . . . even Frosty is of that other gender. Cherry, 6, is on Shirley's right, and Lindy, 5, on her left. Laury, 2, is on my right, and Debby, 4, is holding Frosty.

4. This is what happens when I
try to ride the girls' bicycles.

5. How lucky can any guy be?
(That's Laury.)

(*Credit: Ray Solowinski.*)

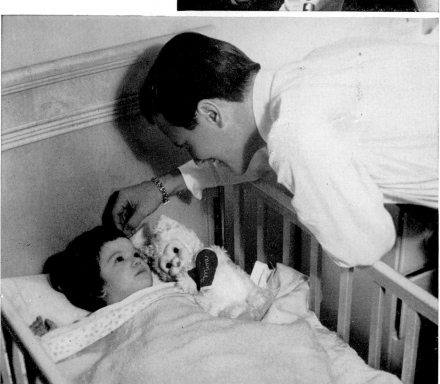

6. If I remember correctly, this was the twenty-eighth take of *Welcome New Lovers*.

(*Credit: Tony Karp.*)

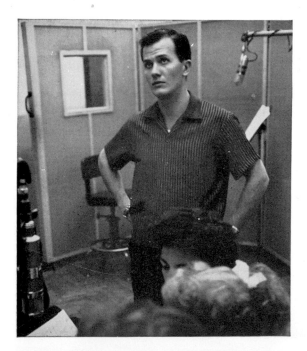

7. Another take?

(*Credit: Tony Karp.*)

8. Listening to playback . . . I didn't like it either. Arty Malvin, choral director; Jack Spina, my personal manager; Randy Wood, President, Dot Records; Mickey Addy, east-coast representative for Dot; Hank Ross, musical coordinator; Mort Lindsey, musical director.

9. What a ham!

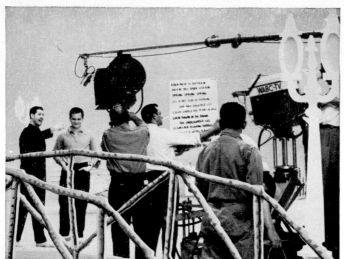

10. Where would we be without our cue cards?

(*Credit: Stuart Smith.*)

11. I'd rather listen to Tyree Glenn than sing

(*Credit: Stuart Smith.*)

12. I'm determined to be a cartoonist.

13. Would you believe it? A fan took this shot.

14. This must be near the end of *Soliloquy*.

behaved people (of all ages) just wait to get behind the
wheel of a car to get even with the world. There's a story
about one couple who had a teen-age son. They were argu-
ing about the best way to make him observe certain simple
civilized rules. "Let's buy Junior his car," the mother suggested. "Do you think that will improve his behavior?" His
dad declared, "No, but it will spread his meanness over a
wider area." Now, I never believed in Junior as anything
but a good hook for a funny line, but sometimes when I'm
pursued bumper-to-bumper, when someone is shining bright
headlights in my eyes, or crowding to pass, I have the feeling
it must be Junior, or Junior grown up, just spreading himself around. And here are a few more occasions where a
brush up on "what you do and how you do it" during your
transition years could help you individually and your generation as a whole to improve Public Relations (you know,
mass bad manners are in some instances responsible for mass
bad reputations—'cause *Bad Manners are interpreted sometimes as Bad Morals*):

In restaurants where the crowd meets—some considera-
tion and courtesy to the waitress?

On busses—public and school—who was that loud show-
off I saw with that little giggler?

As pedestrians—do you saunter, stand in front of cars,
frighten people by jumping off curbs at 'em?

This is the Public You.

Just how *are* your public relations?

And what about personal relations—such things as table
manners, please-and-thank-you, rising for a lady or an older
person, being a good hostess, a good guest?

My first personal contact with you, if we haven't met for-
mally before, would most likely be a handshake, and a handshake is a form of communication. I'll be right down Tennessee honest with you about this opening. If you don't look
at me when you shake hands you leave me cold. I think

maybe you've got something to hide, or there's nobody much home behind those eyes. Furthermore, I shrivel at a flabby paw. I think most people feel the same way. A good firm handshake from a pretty girl can be delightfully feminine. There's no need to convey the idea that you're a wilting petunia now—unless you *are* one, of course. On the other hand, don't be a bone crusher. A nice happy medium—okay —with a straight look?

Now, Mom and Daddy taught us to say "Yes, sir" and "No, ma'am," and it became a habit. "Glad to meet you, sir,"—"Glad to meet you, ma'am," was a must in our household. I still like it. It seems to me especially pleasant in teen-age boys and girls. I always think, "That young'un is well brought up." But I've got news for you. I personally take a dim view of being called "Mr. Boone." To this day I look around to see if Daddy's following me. And I still have a reluctance to call grown-ups by their first names when uninvited and sometimes even when invited, especially if it's someone I respect a lot. Everybody calls Shirley's daddy "Red." I can't. So I call him *"Mr.* Red."

If you wonder about your desirability as a guest—well, check back to the last time you spent the night at a pal's house. Would your young host's Ma be glad to see you again? Or could you have let yourself in for the chop I heard a mother dish out recently to a young friend of her son's who, while recently a guest in her home, had reduced her ice box to a bowwow chest, her kitchen to a shambles, and her youngest daughter, who was trying to make cookies, to tears. The lad came in beaming for a record party and said, "I hope I'm not too late." To which this mother replied, "No, my dear boy, you couldn't come too late."

And as for teen-age guests who make too free with a hostess's home, use the phone without a "May I," put feet and food on the furniture, leave an untidy bathroom, etc., well, it'd be better if they didn't come at all!

A good guest is considerate—and a host or hostess is the same. I know that the guys I remember, the ones I really looked up to were the ones who, when they invited me to their houses, made me feel special. As a house guest, I don't like being fussed over but you can get pretty embarrassed too if you're made to shift for yourself in someone else's home. The middle ground is to make someone feel at home, comfortable—and an honored guest as well.

To me, "bad" manners come from selfishness, a lack of concern about other people. The guy who's always going through the door first, sits down first, eats first; the gal who shoves her way to the head of the line or catches old ladies in revolving doors; they're just not stroking smoothly in the social swim.

If you have any social problems check the Golden Rule as well as Emily Post. Actually the same rules Jesus gave for helping *us* like *us*, the rules for Horse Sense with Wings, will make *others* like *us* as well! The whole point in being successful in your human relations is to decide who and what you really want to be and then make sure you're beaming that personality to the world, loud and clear, through your appearance—your written and spoken words—your manners, public and private—and your ability to make other people know you care. It should come from the heart when you put out your hand and say to a stranger, "It's a pleasure." And it should come from his heart when he is able to say in return, "I'm glad to know you."

5

Parents Are People Too

Sometimes at the end of a long week-end when Shirley, the beautiful partner in the Boone Baby Girl Factory, has been very busy shopping or something and I've been chief baby-sitter, I feel like that lady who received a play-pen as a gift after *her* fourth child arrived. "Thank you for the play-pen," she wrote. "It's a God-send. I sit in it every afternoon and read and the children can't get near me." It's during those moments I want to form the S.P.C.P.

The S.P.C.P. would be a Society for the Prevention of Cruelty to Parents (I can't see why children and animals get *all* the protection). And why don't we have a Be Kind to Parents Week? We have Pickle Week, and Petunia Week, and even Week Week, I think . . . but nobody ever thinks of the poor ol' parent! If none of these things materialize soon, I'll at least write a wistful pamphlet entitled: How to Spoil a Parent and Why Don't You?

I guess the fact that I'm now in the parent camp myself (by four pink noses! (Count 'em!) . . . is bound to influence my thinking a little. But the reason I bring all this up is that I was just thinking . . . since Adam and Eve, no matter what else the teen-ager does or does not have, like freckles, or money, or a big house, or big feet (don't look at me!), most of us started out life with one set of parents. Sometimes we lose one or both and have to make an adjustment, and that's difficult. In recent years a most confusin' complication has set in where some teen-agers acquire three or more parents, two separate sets so to speak, and this over-abundance requires further adjustments and can be even more difficult.

The Parental Me:

When asked what kind of a parent I personally am, I refer the questioners to Shirley who would say firmly that I'm not such a hot one—this week. That's because, like most fathers, I'm not home all the time (on account of bread-winning and the Pat Boone TV Show, movies, etc.) and the little colored pillows on the couch in the den (which the children *are* allowed to play with) looked to me exactly like the little colored pillows on the sofa in the living room (which, it turns out, the children are *not* allowed to play with). When their Mommy returned from a shopping trip last Saturday to find me in charge and colored pillows all over the living room I had to add a belated item to my New Year's Resolutions: I will never again allow the girls to play with the pillows on the sofa in the living room. They *are* different from the pillows on the couch in the den (although it sure beats me, because they *do* look the same). I'm sure a gal will follow Shirley's logic at once—but the guys may share my confusion.

How does a student parent learn these things? By experience. It's obvious that parenthood can't be blue-printed exactly as some experts would have you believe. Any more than the teen-years can. And it ain't easy, pal!

I chuckled when I heard about a harassed papa getting a primary parent lesson from his small son as they hustled up Fifth Avenue the other day. "Pop," demanded the little kid, "how many bricks in that building?" "Well, son, I don't rightly know," said his dad. "Pop, why does the green light mean 'go' and the red light mean 'stop'?" "Well . . . uh . . . now, I'd never thought about it," replied pop. And a few steps later, "Pop, who discovered Central Park?" "Son," said the frantic parent, "we'll have to look that one up—but," giving him a hearty slap on the back, "you keep right on asking questions. Just ask me anything. How else can you learn?"

See what I mean? And only last Sunday I discovered that while it took a mature man to *say* "Divide and Conquer," the instinct for this cunning wisdom is already present in our oldest daughter, Cherry, at age five. Cherry was carrying on a private conversation with several of her dolls, furnishing all the voices herself, and it went about like this:

"Mommy, can—*may* I have a piece of candy?"

A firm voice, "No, Cherry."

"Eva, may I have a piece of candy?"

A pause and then a reluctant voice, "Not now, Cherry."

"Daddy, *can* I have a piece of candy?"

"I guess so." Another pause and then the feminine Dale Carnegie murmured triumphantly, "I love you, Daddy." Now this is tempting. It can turn your head. It's a siren song to male ears. And yet—you know what? When "nice Daddy" was wheedled for the goodies that very afternoon he had to turn monster. He *had* to say, "No, Cherry. Not before supper." That's not easy, believe me.

The blue-print Shirley and I started with for the kind of parents we wanted to be sounded just great. We would encourage independence, self-reliance, good manners, high principles and ideals *without being too strict,* and then encourage self-expression while we dished out love, security, and a sense of belonging, *without spoiling them.* That's a very good blue-print, too. And it sounds so *simple.* Well, being a good parent is simple—just like balancing on a wiggly wire is simple. The trick is merely to put one foot after the other and not lose your balance either way. *Very* simple. But *not* easy.

I think I hear you saying, "These are *your* problems, Pedro. I've got troubles of my own." And you're so right. I only offer this as a Short Prep Course for your own "Operation: Parenthood," which will arrive in due time; and to try to pass along some understanding of what your parents, good, bad, or indifferent, probably went through in getting you as far along as you are.

You've asked me "Do you think parents of today take enough real interest in their children?" and the other way 'round, to which I have to answer honestly—"Some do— some don't," in both cases. And you ask "Can teen-agers by themselves lose the resentment and rebellion that causes adult restrictions?" To which I say—nobody *else* can!

As a 'tween-ager I had a burning desire to get all parents to recognize that most *teen-agers are people—you know, human people—and should be treated as such.* I still have it.

But now, on top of that, as a parent I beg all teen-agers to consider that *parents are people, too,* and need to be treated as such. I notice that even from my little twerps I expect a little understanding, cooperation, affection—and even a mild spoiling, sometimes.

But more of that later. Now let's talk about you and your immediate problem, if any.

The Grown-Up Parent and His Uses:

Do you remember Hortense and Dad and the clothesline that broke?

And Hortense had the Hoss Sense to recognize that Dad could prophesy from his own experience?

Well, *experience dictates most of the reasonable rules made by parents. If you can believe that, the neck (or reputation) you save may be your own.*

I know that the rules you mention in your questions seem *un*reasonable at this moment to you—so let's take a look at them in relation to your future, using for glasses the frame of experience and the lenses of safety and your reputation.

These glasses may cramp your shnozz at first, but you might
see some surprising things!

Take the question, "Why can't I have a car?"—or "Why
can't I date boys who have cars?" If you're in the early teens
(especially if you're a boy) wheels are the symbol of your
independence. I know that they were for me. And *my* mama
and daddy were like yours—they said *no* to my having a car
all the way through high school—even if I could pay for it
myself! They didn't think it was necessary, wise, or safe.
Chee! Wotta grouch!

It seems they didn't believe I personally had enough experience to handle a crate of my own. Do you remember
this one?

> Said a girl from beyond Pompton Lakes,
> "I make the most *stupid* mistakes,
> Now the car's in the hall;
> It went right through the wall,
> When I mixed up the gas and the brakes."

Or this one an insurance salesman friend of mine always
hands a teen-ager who's had a bit of a smash and says it was
all the other guy's fault:

> Here lies the body of Henry J.
> Who died defending his right-of-way,
> He was right all right,
>   As he sped along,
> But he's just as dead as if he'd been wrong.

Well, anyway, adults toss those things at us and about all
we can think of to answer is a sarcastic, "Very funny. But
those corny limericks have nothing to do with me. I'm a *good*
driver!"

Now, I'll tell you a secret. Teen-age drivers in my book
can be the *best*. I've ridden with some who *are* the best (I'd
vote myself as just "pretty good"). But almost without exception they weren't the speed-demon type, either behind
the wheel *or* at owning a car. There's not that big a rush, pal!
That's what experience teaches. Right now you *need* driving

experience—but get it gradually in the family bus under control conditions, until ol' Dad, the guy with the experience, thinks it *wise and safe* for you to own a car and until you can afford one in good condition! And darlin', you with that beautiful young neck—don't be in a hurry to trust it to some fella who's just found that four wheels and an engine go faster than a bicycle—that may be *all* he knows! One buddy of mine, actually a terrific driver, took one chance too many and killed himself, his girl, and three other innocent people in a flaming wreck. It *does* happen!

Of course, if you happen to be one of those rare bugs who can take a pile of junk and build a really good little auto out of it, starting almost from scratch, I say "More power to ya'!" I've never understood a guy who could actually figure out what was wrong with a car and put it back in shape by himself. But I *have* learned that most teen guys who can turn an old jalopy into a "hot rod" are careful drivers who understand that laws are for their protection . . . and they obey 'em! So if you're old enough to have a license and ambitious enough to buy the parts and learn how to put 'em together, I'd whisper in Pop's ear that he oughta let you try it.

You say, "My parents are afraid I can't take care of myself after eleven o'clock." I have a lot of sympathy for you on that score. Mine was an eleven o'clock family and I think I know how Cinderella felt, scared that her pretty duds would turn into rags and her whole evening be ruined because she had to leave the party before everyone else. I know Carol and Artie can stay 'til twelve—and Tom and Mary Ann 'til *one*. If I had my way we'd get all the parents in each age group together and *insist* that they agree on basic rules just like the army. It would save them and *you* strain if *everyone* had to be in at eleven—or twelve—and you never had to leave a going gang.

But pal, I must say something. You may call me a fink, but here goes. When I remember some of the late-night scrapes

I got into (and I wasn't different from any normal guy), the eleven o'clock curfew doesn't sound so stupid any more. I got into my share of mischief as a young fella, and almost without exception, it was in those "after ten" hours. After all, when you come down to it, what is there that's GOOD to do after eleven? So what does that leave for *you?*

And y'know something else? Double-dating used to be fun! I got a kick out of it . . . and now I see the wisdom in it. Like they say, "there's safety in numbers" . . . and "the future you save may be your *own!*"

I know. I know. I'm turning into an ol' creep.' I can see the inconsistency of having fought for the same freedoms you want when I was your age, and now sittin' back and saying blandly, "The restrictions won't do you any harm." But I guess the answer is that I have a little more experience now, and I can see that most of the rules that seem so unreasonable to you now are actually laws of Common Sense which will guard your own health, home-work and reputations. In the meantime, you'll be gaining experience and learning the new rules that govern Adult behavior.

I wouldn't blame you if you felt like the little girl whose older sister scolded her when putting her to bed. "You've had a rotten temper all day long," big sis said.

And the little one, neatly tucked in, came back, "It's temper when it's me an' 'nerves' when it's you."

The best thing I can pass along to you is, "Don't rush." I can stay up all night now if I want to . . . and, y' know, it isn't nearly what it's cracked up to be! Actually, I don't worry too much about your ability to meet these annoyances cheerfully as they come up.

I *do* worry, though, when you say—"They don't trust me." —"They think I'm trying to put something over on 'em." Because this indicates a lack of communication—and if you aren't communicating, you're in trouble. You may lose a pair of great guides who want to help you through the teen-age maze.

Getting in Touch with Parents:

Unfortunately somewhere 'twixt twelve and twenty, it becomes unfashionable to discuss things with parents—while to *agree* with them is practically to acknowledge that you *need* 'em, and some ill-advised teen-agers feel that this puts them back to "child status" again. If you fall for this you get out of touch.

Now, let's be honest. You *do* need 'em. As long as your parents give their support you'll find it safe to make your own decisions. Look what happened to a young friend of mine recently. Ella felt her mother didn't have any confidence in her ability to make her own decisions. A holiday party was coming up and Ella was going to the beauty shop to have her hair styled and set. All the way down in the car she lectured her mom.

"Please let me tell them how I want it done this time," she begged. "Every other time you give the orders and treat me like a *baby*. I'm old enough to know what I want."

So her mother dumped her at the hairdressers and scooted off to do her marketing and then picked Ella up. On the drive home Ella was in tears. She didn't like her new hair-do. It wasn't becoming and she knew it.

"Oh, Mother, this looks terrible," she wailed. "I'll have to go back and have it done over, like it used to be. You can't let me go to the party looking like a *witch!*"

Now, from there on Ella's mother might well have stopped trusting Ella to make her own decisions because somehow they were speaking two different languages. At the surface level Ella was saying, "I don't need you—I need you. I don't want you—I want you. Let me alone—help me." It didn't make much sense.

But Ella's mother could translate. What Ella was really saying was, "Advise me. Don't boss me."

But do we say it? It'd be better if we in the teens spoke a little oftener and more clearly to our elders instead of inventing a secret language and only talking to ourselves—that is, if we want to get our problems settled.

To begin with—try to lay off the jargon when outside your own set. If a boy says, "Slip me some bread, pop," to his Dad, he's apt to get whole wheat instead of money. If you tell your mother you've heard a picture is "ginchy" she'll probably make you miss the best show in town. If your young date says, "Let's make the scene" instead of, "We'd better go now," you may find you won't be allowed out with *him* again.

Now, here's a Boone formula for getting to be trusted—for letting the folks know you're not trying to put anything over. They're general rules for talking things over with parents in a way that gets results. Try it! It worked for me (when I used it!).

First: Be sure you are coming in loud and clear, speaking the same language on the same subject.

Second: Choose the right time and place—do *not* interrupt a business conversation of Dad's, or catch Mom when she's hurrying to get little sister ready for a party. Try turning off the TV once in a while (yes, even my show) and gettin' to know each other.

Third: Don't try to pit one parent against the other. I used to get caught in the middle when *I* tried that! Either pick the one you think has the most wisdom and authority in a particular matter and stand by that one's decision—or call a meeting. You'd be surprised how tickled your parents would be if you matured enough to know that two heads are better than one—and that "divide and conquer" doesn't work in the home.

Fourth: Try to be reasonable, intelligent, and to the point in your requests or complaints. Remember the fisherman in the fairy tale who hooked the magic fish and by increasing requests raised his wife and himself from a hovel to a castle. But when his wife wanted the sun and moon to obey her they found themselves back in their shack again!

One last bit of advice. *Spoil* your parents from time to

time. You like a little spoiling, don't you? I remember that my Mamma was always very demonstrative. She likes to kiss and hug us and say, "I love you." As little children we liked it. But as we got older that sort of embarrassed us. It always stuck in my throat. Most teeners tend to shy away from any outward emotion or affection. Yet the few times when, as a teen-ager, I would give her a kiss and say, "I love you, Mama," tears came to her eyes.

My advice is to thaw a bit . . . melt the chill. Don't be too "mature for that stuff." Kiss your Mom. Pat your sisters and brothers (not *too* hard). Ask your Dad on a date—ball game, show, or otherwise. Just you two.

It works wonders, those displays of affection, 'cause basically, real love (not sentiment) is the answer to almost all the human relations problems of this old world

Extreme-Type Parents—and What to Do About Them:

The too strict parent and the over protective parent don't allow their teen-ager to make his blunders at a normal rate of speed. They tend to slow you down and, while not dangerous (the only danger is if you bolt and butt your head into a wall or permit yourself to be filled with resentment) certainly this is a tough row to hoe.

Their motives would seem to be fear, a genuine lack of trust not only in the teen-age but the older world—and the best, in fact the *only* advice I can give you is to work hard on communicating with 'em and to do everything you can to build their trust. Defiance or rule-breaking with such as these only confirms their worst suspicions and tightens the bit in your mouth. There's no doubt that if your parents are really unreasonable, you're going to have to be *more* reasonable and mature than the average young person.

The too lenient or "indifferent" parent, on the other hand, can be the *most dangerous*. They withdraw with all their experience and leave you alone on the field.

There were a couple of kids, friends of one of my sister's,

whom I watched struggle along with a set of parents who just dropped the reins and let 'em run. The girl had such a bad reputation by the time she graduated from high school that she had to go husband-hunting in another state and even that wasn't far enough. The boy, after being kicked out of several schools, both public and private, wound up in a wild automobile wreck in which one of the passengers was killed. Finally, the parents had to face the realization that they had given love without guidance, freedoms without supervision. The saddest part was that their children suffered most.

Now, I want to say right here that my Mama was *really* alert. She seemed to know every second where I was, what I was up to and who I was with. She had a seventh sense and seemed to know if I was just *planning* to do something that was out of order and *that always gave me pause to think— and if we pause to think we usually come up with the right decision.* (That's Horse Sense.)

I'm not saying it didn't irk me to have my family so interested in *everything* I did. But today I'm grateful. Now, it's absolutely true that you do not have to "go to the dogs" because *your* parents are indifferent. But you'll have to work twice as hard. Grow up faster. That is, if you want a happy life.

The decision here is all yours. You can use problem parents for an excuse to be miserable all your life or you can open your eyes right now, adopt some of the rules imposed on other guys and gals you admire—stick close to your Heavenly Father—and *bring yourself up to be the strongest of all.*

My friend, you with an extra parent (because of death, divorce, or remarriage) —work hard on getting in touch. The wicked step-mother is a fairy tale. If you can "get in touch" you can have something pretty special. If you aren't in touch, are you the one who did the shutting out? I feel for you, pal, and know you have extra problems, maybe, but you can and should be happy, too.

When we come to the deep problems-with-parents—the kids who have to contend with a mother or father ill on alcohol, morally or spiritually ill, we—all of us—have a job to do. We have to open our normal world to them. To show them what a joy it is to live in the sunshine of goodness and right. To help them overcome humiliation, shame, defiance, the old chip-on-the-shoulder. We've got to encourage their loyalty and not invade the privacy they keep around their dark secret world. Try to draw them *out* of it. But for you, again, if this is your situation, I know there is every hope—for you *have* a Heavenly Father—and you, too, can bring yourself up. And to help your parents—remember—love works wonders with problem parents, too.

I'd like to offer you, whatever your story is, a prayer from my scrapbook—a prayer that can be used for problem parents, or daily problems, or any teen-age situation. It isn't an old one. It isn't a new one. It isn't long, either. But it's powerful:

> God, grant me the serenity to accept the things I cannot change;
> The courage to change the things I can.
> And the wisdom to know the difference.

6

Can This Be Love?

"My daughter is 'going steady' with three boys at once. Is that normal these days?" This question from a puzzled mother really knocked me for a loop.

All that I could reply was—not that I know of! Cupid must have shot her with a machine gun. Or she's had a bad attack of that traditional teen virus, Spring Fever, and it's gone to her head. Romance, of course, isn't a teen-age exclusive. Even old married fogies like the P. Boones have occasional attacks of it when they go wandering in the woods hand-in-hand, feeling light-hearted and nutty, remembering with many chuckles and much happiness the teen-time of our spring love (only six years ago—or is it seven already?).

But it's from teen-timers that the questions about Romance come pouring in. "When will I be old enough to date?" "Should I let a boy kiss me the first time we go out?" "I want to go steady but my girl is against it—what do you think?" "How can I be more attractive to boys?" "How do you ask the most popular girl for a date?" "How do I know if this is real love?"

So I've dug into a private stock of memories to see if we can't come up with some tips that may help you through these intoxicating, exciting, but so, so confusin' first dating days.

Love in Bloom:

I sing about love ("Tutti Frutti" and "Ain't That A Shame" to the contrary). Singers have to believe in romance because it's just about the favorite theme of poets, lyric writers and music makers. I cast my vote for Cupid with just about every song I sing. And this is a strange twist of fate, because I've already told you that I couldn't seem to bring myself to mention the word at home, or even *let on* that I really loved my own folks! And Shirley and I went steady for almost a year before I'd break down and say "I love you!" But the love *was* there in my heart all along, as it is in yours, and I honestly think that singing my songs has made it easier for me to break down and let my loved ones and friends know I care.

Do you know why I think it's important enough to sing about? Because, in musical logic, it's love that makes the world go round, like Mr. Como's songwriter thought to say before me. Love of God. Love of country. Love of friends. And that very special kind of love, the love you'll feel for your One-And-Only when he or she comes down the road. That kind leads to marriage, and marriage leads to families, and families make nations, but always at the core of the nation is a partnership, a boy and girl who loved each other both wisely and well, who became husband and wife, and then father and mother.

That's the Far Goal of your Dating Days! You're already in the preliminary bouts, as Rocky Graziano would say.

The basic moves we have to cover are simple. The footwork, you might say. We usually start those first, tentative approaches toward the opposite sex with the attitude: "I love *me,* and I'm going to take good care of *me* and see that *I'm* properly treated and safe and have a good time."

Then one day along comes someone who smiles at us in a funny little way and we grow a bit. We think: "I like *you* because you like *me,* and I'll be safe with you." Now we're gettin' someplace—we have the beginning of a twosome.

But it takes a lot more growing before we reach the day when we can finally say: "I love *you,* and I'm going to take good care of you and see that you're properly treated and safe and that, no matter what happens to me, all is well with *you* forever." Strangely enough, in that instant when we forget ourselves, when we put someone else in first place, we become winners. That's what we call—True Love (there's a good song title).

The journey toward love starts quite naturally and sanely with our first date.

Dating Daze:

Once, in the 20th Century-Fox commissary (mess hall), I overheard a producer outlining a simple, sweet young love story to a writer. This, he said, was the screen play he wanted: "Boy-meets-girl. Boy-loves-girl. Boy-loses-girl. Boy-gets-girl. They live happily ever after." That's a dandy, isn't it? And don't you wish it took about that long and was that easy?

But of course it isn't. And when you come right down to it, who wants to miss the fun of doing it the real way? Boy, I wouldn't have missed those first dating days, the going steady and breaking up, the jealousy and heartache and happiness for *anything!*

Usually, though, it starts just as the producer has it figured. Boy-meets-girl (and, of course, girl-meets-boy at about the same time unless someone forgets the script). But the next question is, when do boy-and-girl-notice-each-other-and-start-dating? Now, I'm going to answer that one just like an adult and say sagely—that depends. Well, natch! A boy with an avid interest in sports and a hatful of hobbies may not notice a girl *as a girl* for quite a while. That doesn't mean he's a drag. And some girls go into their junior or senior year in high school without paying too much attention to boys. This doesn't make her a drip.

Sometimes these slow starters move into the dating game at the end of the fifth inning and start scoring big with the first pitch. They've gone through the shy, awkward, self-conscious stage and arrived in the game pretty well seasoned and all set to hit home-runs. So don't worry if you're not in there on the first pitch. Your innings will surely come.

Take the case of Ann Wolfe, Shirley's good friend during her days at West Hi in Nashville. The first couple of years at West, Ann didn't date much at all. A big reason was her weight. Toward the end of her sophomore year, a doctor discovered she had a thyroid problem. He treated it and she began immediately to lose pounds.

I didn't know her then. I first met her when I sang at the Miss Nashville Contest. Guess who was Miss Nashville that year? Ann Wolfe. Guess who was Runner-Up to Miss Tennessee that year? Ann Wolfe. Guess who went on to be one of the prettiest and most popular stewardesses American Airlines ever had? And who married a handsome newspaperman? You tell me.

Now if you belong to the group who starts noticing the opposite sex early, at the thirteen, fourteen, and fifteen year level (pre-driver's license), you'll operate under some handicaps for a while, and you'll find the ground rules in those early innings pretty restrictive. That's okay. Stick with 'em, if you don't want to strike out before the big game is even under way.

Looks like we're at the point of "who asks who" for the date and "how" you ask. Here, whether you're a pre-driving 'tween-ager or a heap-pilot, the rules are the same.

Generally speaking, Miss America, don't seek out boys and suggest that they take you out, even in Leap Year! You'll scare the boy off if you move rapidly in his direction. And he'll outrun you because he hates to be caught. It's the nature of the beast. He wants to chase *you!* On the other hand, ma'am, it's a valuable thing for you to know when to stop running and how to do it gracefully.

Take the case of Miss Sheila, now. She'd kept an eye on a very shy fellow for a long spell. She had patience enough to match his bashfulness and finally, one night, he gathered all his courage together, sneaked up behind her and covered her eyes with his hand. She recognized the voice that whispered, "I'm gonna kiss you if you can't tell who this is in three guesses." Promptly she guessed, "George Washington —Thomas Jefferson—Abraham Lincoln." And that, my lass, is how to catch a fellow while standing still.

In asking for any date the same basic rules apply. First, try to have something interesting to suggest, something you think this particular person will enjoy. Then, either by telephone or in person, say frankly, "Would you like to come with me to the rodeo at the junior college on Saturday?" Or, "The basketball game next Friday night?" Or, "A costume party for most of our class at Patty Dailey's home on the sixth?" Try not to say, "How about a date Friday night?" Or, "Are you busy on the fourteenth?" I knew one high school queen who really jolted 'em by answering, "I can't tell yet. What did you want to do?"

And what about kissing? When? Who? How? Here's an area where, in the last book, you didn't think I "went deep enough." So? Now! Here goes— First, there is "kissing," and *kissing,* and KISSING. Mixed-up? Yes. Crazy? No. I'm for two of them at the right time and in the right place and with the right person. "Kissing" is what kids do as a mark of affection, or as a part of pretending to be grown-up. Usually the pre-teens regard it in some odd ways.

A few days ago, Cherry came inside laughing. "That little Paulie McAuliff—he's so funny! He won't let me kiss him." She was really tickled.

"Well, what in the world are you trying to kiss him for?"

I asked, hearing wedding bells already ringing faintly in the future.

"I just wanted to," she explained matter-of-factly. "Albert lets me kiss *him* any time I want to." And off she went to beg Mommy for a Fudgecicle.

Of course I'm not worried about five-year-old Albert Champon, from next door. As for Cherry, she may catch a cold, but that's about all.

I remember a ten-year-old named Joe in a TV show once, who was really bugged over girl problems and was discussing them with a couple of pals. "I've walked to school with Margie three times," he said, "and carried her books. I bought her ice cream sodas twice. Now do you think I oughta kiss her?"

"Naw, you don't need to," said one of his pals after thinking a bit. "You've done enough for her already."

A "kiss," in this particular frame of mind, will probably never occur and if it does it will be an embarrassing but innocent token of affection. But *kissing* is something else again.

Kissing, and my 'tween-age readers will dig what I mean, is an important part of "making out," it's our first attempt at adult love-making, and too often is the spark that ignites big trouble; it's not remarkably sweet or innocent, nor is it all right in view of KISSING.

KISSING is something that belongs to the One-And-Only, that one you hope to love some day, both wisely and well—and you'd better start right now taking care of you for that ONE. Don't accept a cheap substitute that might spoil the real thing when it comes along.

I mentioned earlier that I felt sorry so many kids your age seem to have very difficult decisions forced on you too soon. Believe me, when I hear teen-agers short of marriageable age (let's put this at eighteen as the earliest economically and physically in most cases) "frankly and publicly discussing" where and whom and how to "neck" or "pet"—"to-neck-or-not-to-neck—to-pet-or-not-to-pet"—"how to handle a guy's passes,"—I hurt a little. It isn't that sex should be a taboo subject. As we've already agreed, it's Horse Sense to get straight, honest, intelligent adult information about it from your parents, your minister, your doctor, or some qualified expert.

It can be equally damaging to "know nothing" or to get your information from a pal and "know what isn't so."

But to find that rushing into this dangerous experimental area is so common that it can be "frankly discussed" in parties, on panels, or in mixed-teen-groups, makes me a little sad. I *am* proud of the stands you take on these things. But I *do wish* our society protected you a little longer from running this obstacle course.

Believe your buddy Pat, "making out" in all its forms spells danger to the light heartedness, the gaiety, the fun of young love. And I can promise you, Lady Friend, that it's not a real addition to your popularity, your reputation, *or* your Big Love, when it comes along. If you have to resort to it in any form to be "popular," then you "ain't got what it takes."

The teens are almost split, date-wise, into pre-car and the car dating days. Cars make a difference. Kimball Young, a noted sociologist, said once that cars had done more to change the pattern of courtship than anything that had happened in two thousand years. Now you and I know about cars. We know that when Tom asked his insurance man why there are fewer railroad accidents than automobile accidents the insurance expert was voicing as much truth as humor when he replied: "Well, it might be because the engineeer isn't always huggin' the fireman!"

We know that, once we've reached the age where dating in cars is allowed, we're more on our own and more responsible for our conduct than we have ever been before. You, and only you, can decide on your car conduct, but since you've asked me I'll tell you what Shirley and I will one day tell our little lambs. *Cars are a method of transportation. When they're not gettin' you around, they're gettin' you in trouble.* If you want to "set a-while," try using your own living room or porch. I'll guarantee Mom and Pop will make themselves scarce if you'll explain this decision.

In fact, if your principles are high, if you're dependable and reliable, if you state openly where you're going, with whom, what time you'll be home (and, sweetheart, introduce the poor lug to your folks!); in other words, if you show your family common courtesy and sweet reasonableness by asking to do only what's appropriate to your age, you won't have a "family problem." You'll probably have a lot of support with your dating. Try it!

Now let's zero in on two last areas where you've asked my ideas about specific rules: Blind Dates and Pick Ups. Well, now, Cooga Mooga's answer to Dear Abby has pretty definite ideas on both of these. They go like this. Pick Ups—NEVER! Are you kidding? Blind Dates—with discretion. When I say, "Blind Dates with discretion," I mean that a date you haven't met, arranged by a friend you trust, to go some place or do something your common sense tells you is fun can enlarge your circle of friends. "Pick Ups NEVER!" means just that. Oh, brother!—not under any circumstances. No pick-ups in a car because you need a ride, or because the car is cute, or the boys or girls are cute. No telephone pick-ups. You never heard of that? Well, one nut got a real shock when he dialed a number and said, "Hello, Mabel, can I see you tonight?" And the girl's voice said, "Sure thing, Bill, come on over." Our pal gulped, "Hey, this isn't Bill." And the girl said, "And I'm not Mabel, but come anyway."

But wait! Suppose you—if you're a girl—notice the boys but the boys never notice you? Or the other way 'round. Then all these rules are pretty useless, aren't they? But there *are* techniques for getting noticed at the right time by the right guy or gal. So don't go 'way.

Are You Date-Bait?

Let's start by saying: if you don't light yourself up, you'll stay in the dark. *Appearance* is certainly one factor in attracting a boy's or girl's attention in the first place—and trying to be always neat, clean and appropriately dressed will make a date proud to be seen with you.

When a teen-age boy was asked in an English vocabulary test for a one word description of "love of man-kind," he answered, "Woman!"

He didn't say "Imitation Boy nor "sloppy Jane" and the reverse is true, too. The "love of Womankind" is "Man," not "sloppy Joe," the oversized kid, nor "Winsome Wilfred" with the ducktail and Vassar wave. The big movie stars that the girls scream over are guys like Clark Gable and Cary Cooper —the he-men! To answer one of your teen-age journalists' questions, "Are American Girls Losing Their Femininity By Following Fads," I would say truthfully I do think American girls are in more danger of losing their femininity by following fads than boys are of losing their masculinity. The reason is simple. Except for the few who still cling to the duck-tail instead of the flat-top I think men of fashion have become *more masculine* through the years—remember there was a time when the male had a corner on ringlets, lace cuffs, satin, plumed hats, and powdered hair!

But since 1900 women's fashions have become *more masculine, too!* And part of the male population has been protesting right along. I remember a clipping my Mama had, written fifty years ago when ladies were still addicted to the bustle and side saddle, indicating how shocked were the males of conservative Boston when the females began their invasion of the world of pants. This was published in a Boston paper in 1901:

> Oh, we might have heard serenely,
> Of the overthrow of kings,
> Oh the flight of many comets,

Of the fall of Saturn's rings;
But the world seems sadly muddled,
Things have surely gone amiss
ly
bold ride
women their
Boston nags
the like
Since this.

Whew! What would they have thought of the Blue Jean Brigade or the Slack Set?

The truth is that appearance is certainly one important item in being attractive and the trick lies in three little words; Be Your Sex, but that's not the whole secret of attraction.

The whole truth is that, except for a fortunate few who just naturally have it made from the minute they uncork that first smile, in the early, delicate days of first dating *everybody's* a little awkward and self-conscious in some way. It takes different forms, but most folks are in that beginning phase where they say defensively, "I love *me* and I'm going to take good care of myself."

The keenest thing you can do is to recognize your trouble for what it is, get *your* mind off *you* and be the one to penetrate that wall of self-defense. A warm out-going friendliness—an honest kindness—is a better magnet than glamor appeal.

I remember Joan, the first girl I noticed in high school. She wasn't a real doll but she was BRIGHT. Boy, she sparkled! We had an English class together and she was at least bright enough to always laugh at my jokes (all real killers, 'cause I stole 'em regularly from the Bob Hope radio show). She was always interested in the grades I got, cheered if they were good, sympathized if they weren't so hot. I liked her because she liked me. Remember state two? Nothing mushy or gushy—she was my friend because I felt she was

on my team and I didn't have to prove anything. I wasn't
dating much then but I did carry her books when we walked
together—and if we'd been a little older I would have taken
her to a movie, or some big deal like that.

She certainly wasn't my O-A-O. She wasn't even a potential steady, really. We were much too young and she wasn't
it anyway. But I liked her a lot. And that's how dating starts.

Now I know, both from my own experience and from talking to my buddies, what a guy looks for in a date. And I've
conned the most attractive girl I know (*my* O-A-O) into co-
operating on what she and her girl friends liked (we'll
exclude white buck shoes and a peculiar type singing voice
since this might be considered a personal eccentricity) and
here's a guide-test so you can evaluate where you stand.

DATE-BAIT TEST

Boys and Girls Answer

Yes____	No____	(1)	Are you enthusiastic about most activities, be they shows, parties, the bowling alley or a Sunday afternoon hike? Do you *expect* to have a good time?
Yes____	No____	(2)	Do you take pains to look your best and dress as neatly and appropriately for a movie as for a party, for a hike as for ice skating?
Yes____	No____	(3)	Are you considerate of the gal or guy you came with? Do you hide your feelings even if you wish you were there with the little red-head from Camden or the new football star?
Yes____	No____	(4)	*Do you listen?* Are you honestly interested in what your date has to say; or do you try to overhear what they're laughing about in the corner?
Yes____	No____	(5)	Are you informed? Can you talk intelligently about any of the things that interest the opposite sex, or both sexes, such as music—cars—

sports—school politics—world affairs—etc.?

Yes_____ No_____ (6) How are your manners? Do you treat your date as someone special to you for the evening? Do you treat others as you would have them treat you? Are you prompt? (I bomb out here! Why'd you have to mention promptness?)

Yes_____ No_____ (7) Are you trusting and trustworthy? No jealousy and no possessiveness on the one hand—no flirting on someone else's time on the other. No using this date as a stepping stone to bigger things.

Yes_____ No_____ (8) Are you a good sport? Do you join in willingly no matter what's going on so long as it doesn't violate your personal principles?

Yes_____ No_____ (9) Are you willing to place principles above personalities and temporary popularity even if it seems to hurt at the time? (*My friend, this is a very important one if you intend to have any solid, worthwhile admiration over the long pull.*)

Yes_____ No_____ (10) Do you refrain from gossiping about others to your date? (Because he or she can't help suspecting they'll be next on your Yakety-Yak list.)

Yes_____ No_____ (11) Do you refrain from making fun or criticizing the guys or gals you've been out with, even to close pals? (If it gets around and you have this reputation no one will want to risk taking you out.)

For Girls Only

Yes_____ No_____ (12) When you have a choice, do you choose *the boy you like best* instead of the biggest spender or the owner of the flashiest car or the one who invites you to the best social event?

Yes_____ No_____ (13) Are you budget-kind? Will you smile as sweetly if taken by bus to a nice neighborhood theater to see a good movie, as if you were escorted in a car to see the *same* movie at a plush downtown palace? Do you watch for that worried look at the drive-in or ice-cream bar and take a cherry coke instead of a banana split?

Yes_____ No_____ (14) Do you make the boy feel comfortable and presentable by proudly introducing him to your folks?

For Boys Only

Yes_____ No_____ (12) Do you try to think up interesting, different things to do? Lolling around listening to records or watching TV is fine part of the time. It's okay, too, if you've taken a girl out several times to ask her once in a while what she wants to do. But generally speaking it's up to you to find out the girl's tastes and match them with your imagination, transportation and ready cash. (Mainly imagination, huh?)

Yes_____ No_____ (13) Do you treat your dates like grown ladies—with that extra bit of courtesy? (Even if she's only half-an-hour out of pony-tail and saddle shoes? Even if she isn't out of them yet?) Man, they eat it up!

Yes_____ No_____ (14) Do you remember that day before yesterday, teasing was the best way you knew to get a girl's attention? Do you try to control the urge now? (You won't outgrow the temptation over-night but resist it as much as you can.) A little's enough.

Now for your Date-Rate, Date-Bait!

If you've answered "yes" to twelve or more you've got what it takes. You'll rate high with the opposite sex "like wow!"

If you've answered "yes" to 9-11, you're still in the safety zone. You shouldn't have any trouble.

If you've answered "yes" to 5-8, you'd better try a little harder—quick!

If you've only managed a "yes" to 1-4 . . . well, even your best friend can't stand you! Get busy on an inventory and see *why* you feel as you do—and do something about it, pronto!

The Steady Picture:

Now—the all-important question—is this love? And if so, "should we go steady?"

First, let's take the question "is this love?" I'm afraid no one can answer this but you. But if you've gone and "fallen in love *at first sight*" you may have a lot of pieces to pick up at second or third or thirty-third glance.

What's your hurry? Why not take a good look?

Here's the point. I believe we *grow* into love, starting from that spark of attraction and widening as we get to know each other. At least that was the way it happened with Mrs. B and me.

Now, you've asked "What's your opinion of teen-agers going steady—and do you believe it helps or hinders their life?"

It seems to me going steady can be a late-teen-age method of trying to find out if this growth is really taking place; while in the early teens it's usually a game and not a very permanent or meaningful one. It's real at the time, but lasts about one inning. Gets rained out.

There are pros and cons to the "steady" picture, and the "pros" seem to me to apply only to teen-agers old enough to think they're almost ready for a formal engagement to marry. They may believe they have found that all important *one*.

If this is true, then it should really be a testing time. A time to test the quality of your companionship, your quarrel-rate, your ability to adjust to differences, your similarities in vital areas like aims, ideals, religion, family life. Then it has point and purpose. Shirley and I went "serious-steady" before we were married.

But remember, I "went steady" twice before the real thing came along! Looking back I really believe that going steady is often the fastest way to kill the relationship. One or the other is usually watching to see who's looking where, and who's getting tired of whom, and pretty soon, under this strain, everybody wants out—but that's easier said than done.

And, so Shirley tells me, it's sometimes hard for a girl who's labeled as "going steady" to get back in the swim again. A fellow can just begin to ask other girls out—but the girl may find it more difficult.

Besides, continued intimacy—"getting to know each other very well"—can lead to a relaxed familiarity where those moral and ethical standards on "making out" waver and even fall. I don't say it *would,* but the danger is greater and the decisions more frequent. And certainly this wouldn't *help* your future life.

Another angle to consider, too, in trying to decide this all-important question of whether to go steady or not would be based on motive. If you must admit to one of these as your honest reason for going steady, my advice is—*BEWARE!*

1. *Is it laziness or fear?* Are you too tired or too afraid to compete? Do you just like the security of always having a ready-made, well-trained date on hand?

2. *Are you a reformer?* Do you feel that going steady will be a "good influence" on him or her? Help "change" them? If you feel someone needs changing it's a poor foundation for a loving relationship.

3. *Are you a scalp collector?* Do you go steady with this one, that one, and maybe three at a time?

4. *Do you (girls) feel motherly towards the boy?* If so, go ahead and mother him—and a mother's duties romantically consist in advising him about other girls. Be his best friend.

5. *Do you like the feeling of possessiveness or domina-*

tion? "This girl is *mine!* All mine!" "I can make my boy friend do anything I want."

6. *Are you grateful?* Gratitude is a wonderful emotion. But just because he or she "has been so kind to me" doesn't make that one the love of your life.

The best recipe I could offer for the ideal teen-age relationship during the budding of romance would not be to "go steady." It has a heavy feel—an almost-married attitude. Trapped! Marriage is beautiful when it comes marrying time! No one recommends it more heartily than I. And in the next chapter we'll talk about marriage.

But to have all the joy of teen-time dating we need a lighter touch—a touch of youth! Don't rush through your romantic springtime. Enjoy it! You won't pass this way again! Be gay. Be enthusiastic. Above all, be young and innocent—in the very best sense of the words. And if you're interested in everything and in everyone, you'll develop an understanding heart—plus an ability to truly love, both wisely and well, that *One-And-Only* who will surely come along.

7

Happily Ever After

And so they were married and lived happily ever after—
Where have I heard that before?

Would a child's fairy tale be a fairy tale if it didn't end that way? And today don't most of our novels and TV shows and movies end that way (the romantic phrase for it in Hollywood is "Clinch—*Cut!*")? All of which leads to the conclusion that a Happy Marriage is a very worthwhile goal for almost all folk. And being myself a partner in just such a real life drama, I can't recommend it too highly. In short, "why *not,* bubbala?"

But the contents of the Ol' Mail Bag from time to time set Your Boy Pat awonderin' just how far some teeners have grown beyond the fairy tale and movie concept of *how* this ideal is to be achieved. "A Prince and Princess," some letters seem to say, "enough True Love—a Song for two for romantic flavoring—a Moon—a fast beating pulse—the words and promises of a Magic Ceremony—plus a sprinkling of Luck" and out will pop a well blended Happy Marriage.

Oh, it sounds swoony, for sure, and I can hear the millions sigh, "Ain't Love Grraand!"

I don't want to be the old-fashioned egg-beater that puts lumps in the batter, or the lemon extract that sours your sweet-dream concoction, but as a man who's "been there"

15. What a beautiful spot . . . the Mirabelle Gardens in Salzburg, Austria.

16. They were wonderful to us in Stockholm, Sweden . . . Here's a puzzle for you, try to find Shirley in this picture.

17. We ran into one of our fan clubs in Paris.

18. and 19. One of the biggest thrills on our trip to Europe was meeting our foster boys. We met Franz Stelzner, 12, in Salzburg, Austria (top), and little Giuseppi Marcelli, 8, in Venice, Italy (bottom). Shirley and I adopted these boys under the Foster-parent plan three years ago. This was our first meeting after much correspondence.

20. Shirley and I . . . from Nashville, Tennessee, to Paris, France.

21. I was a split second too late. He scored the two points. Wendell Niles, Jr., Len Gochman, and Bob Crystal.

(*Credit: Tony Karp.*)

22. Ingemar Johansson looked a little bit too serious, so I quit.

(*Credit: Wagner-International Photos.*)

23. That older gentleman with Paul Anka, Frankie Avalon, and Bobby Darren, is me.

(Credit: Wagner-International Photos.)

24. Carlo Menotti, my singing coach, gives me some rough exercises but . . . they work.

(Credit: Stuart Smith.)

25. President Eisenhower's surprise resulted from my answer to his question—"You have four daughters? How old are you?" The occasion was the presentation to the President of a Bible at the beginning of National Bible Week. On the President's left is H. E. Humphreys, Jr., Chairman, U. S. Rubber Co. My answer was: "Twenty-four.")

26. Ouch, Daddy, says Frosty . . . Debby is squeezing me.

(Credit: Ray Solowinski.)

27. Me at my dramatic best saying "Au Revoir" for now.

(like seven years worth!) I've got to warn you that while love is certainly Grraand, "ever after" is a looong time. And the above formula, which is certainly part of the frosting, is just no guarantee of a whole cake. To believe in this kind of magic is to walk right into disappointment and even heartbreak.

Day after tomorrow, or at least one day soon, you're gonna be a hopeful bride or a nervous groom. And while it's true that it takes only love, the price of a license, and some magic words to make a wedding legal, it takes a whole lot more to make it a Happy Marriage.

Here's a typical letter that came in—the kind that really sends your Mail Bag Einstein into a tailspin. It was written by an engaged gal—this differs from the "steady-going" type by one small sparkler on her left hand and the fact that she and her boy friend actually have the altar in their sights. Wendy writes:

> "So we're young, like my family says. I say what's better than being in love while we're young, with a whole life together ahead of us? Mom and Dad keep asking me what 'kind of a marriage' I want—what Rod and I 'expect to *make* of our life together.' We haven't really thought much about that stuff. If we're truly in love that'll work itself out. Don't you think the important thing is to get off on the right foot? I *do* know exactly the kind of wedding I want."

Wendy's wedding plans call for the whole treatment, boy. She wants to be a June bride married in a sunny garden (Madison Square would do), radiant in bridal white with veil and orange blossoms, with a whole platoon of bridesmaids, ushers, and a best man traipsing along behind. There's to be a three-story cake at the reception, a cloudburst of rice at the exit, a glorious honeymoon and on their return her new hubby will lug her over the threshold.

Then, because they're in love and have gotten "off on the right foot" with a "proper" wedding, Wendy (she has wide, trusting eyes—I just know it) expects the "happily ever after" to work *itself* out.

Does that sound logical to you?

On the level, and despite the fact that Shirley and I eloped (for reasons which we'll discuss later) I do believe that a beautiful wedding *is* a romantic way to start married life. No gettin' around it— When Shirley's sister, Jenny, was married in our garden a couple of summers ago we had a lot of fun fixing up the trimmings. I even provided the "song or two for flavoring." And there were happy tears all over the place—mostly Shirley's and mine! All this has its own kind of sweet magic plus memory magic. But to me it seems more than risky to mistake the frosting for the cake, to depend on "trimmings" to get you off on the right foot.

Did you ever wonder where some of our bridal customs come from? The preference for the month of June, orange blossoms, the rice trick, etc.? I did. And for Wendy's information, as well as yours and mine, I looked into it. Hang on.

Demons and Omens:

Let's start with that diamond engagement ring every girl hopes to latch onto. Why a diamond instead of a ruby or a pearl or a nice inexpensive rhinestone? Because the diamond, as late as the Middle Ages, was supposed to get its sparkle from the "fires of love," to be good magic against the Evil Eye, and a symbol of permanence 'cause it never wears out. (A "diamond is forever"—remember?) The wedding ring itself represented the circle—symbol of eternity, foreverness. And why are both to be worn on the third finger of the left hand? Because in ancient times the heart, which they'd discovered to be on the left side of the body, was regarded as the center of emotions, and the Egyptians thought that a special vein (love's vein) ran directly from the heart to that fourth finger on a fast express! Later a Roman scholar wrote that the wedding ring must always be worn on that finger to keep love from escaping from the heart. Imagine love leaking out your finger!

June was always the most popular month for brides. This was because in Roman mythology, Juno, the goddess of women, was its patron saint and supposedly blessed all weddings taking place then. June's stock really went up when to this was added the idea "happy the bride that the sun shines on," because the sun's light would bring many children. (Wow! What if *we'd* been married in June?) It had its practical aspects in England, too, 'cause here, up until the middle of the sixteenth century, they followed the custom of the Far East and married off the young folk outside, usually at the door of the church. Certainly a bride exposed by custom to the elements would be far happier (and prettier) on a sunshiny day in June than in a November hailstorm!

Bridal white signifies purity to many of us, but there's also an Old Wives' tale which versified the fate brought on the bride by her selection of color for her gown:

> Married in white, you've chosen aright,
> Married in red, you'd be better off dead,
> Married in yellow, ashamed of the fellow,
> Married in blue, your lover is true,
> Married in green, ashamed to be seen,
> Married in black, you'll ride in a hack,
> Married in pearl, you'll live in a whirl,
> Married in pink, your spirits will sink,
> Married in brown, you'll live out of town.

We're stuck with the ushers and the bridesmaids because of an old Roman Law that required ten witnesses at a wedding, which would be legally sensible, I guess. But the *real* purpose was to deceive any evil spirits by dressing the bridesmaids like the bride and the groomsmen like her intended. This way, should a jealous demon envy the happiness that lay before the marrying pair and want to make trouble, he'd have a "devil" of a time figuring out which was the woosome twosome—dig? Oh, the good ol' days! What sneaks they were!

The best man had a slightly more modern origin and a practical purpose which he's no longer called on to fulfill (at least I've never seen him try it!). True, today the best man serves the useful function of hanging onto the ring for the shaky groom. But in an older day when the groom often had to capture his bride by *force,* he required a very good friend, in fact the "best man" he could find, to stand and fight off her relatives while he cut out with his lady.

The honeymoon came into popularity at this same time. This was natural because it was really necessary for the young couple to dash away from her friends and relatives and for the groom to keep her hidden until her family either gave up the search or agreed gracefully to the marriage. The actual term *honeymoon* came from a custom that decreed that one month after the wedding, while the moon was going through its shrinking phases, the newly married couple drank mead, a wine made from honey.

Now, according to the sages of the ages, here's the lowdown on orange blossoms, veils, cakes, and rice. The orange tree, so thought the Orientals, has much good magic. It's evergreen, so it's a natural as a symbol of love everlasting.

It also bears blossoms and fruit at the same time, a talent which makes the orange blossom a fine "omen" for weddings (no explanation needed). The wedding veil is thought to be a sample-size relic of the bridal canopy once carried over the heads of both bride and groom to ward off the Evil Eye (boy, they *were* suspicious!). And rice thrown at the departing couple is what's left of an ancient Hindu and Chinese religious rite where rice, their chief food, was showered on the couple to insure health and prosperity, not to mention an additional value if any jealous spirits were in the neighborhood. If a selfish spook were hovering about, the rice offering might serve as a bribe. The goblins never had it so good!

The wedding cake seems an outgrowth of the playful old Roman custom of breaking a sort of cake over the bride's head to bring her wealth and joy. Picture that, nowadays! A bit of the cake was picked up by each guest to share in her good luck.

The Roman groom customarily carried his bride over the threshold to make sure she didn't trip, an ill omen if done on one's wedding day, and also because she might forget to enter on her right foot and thus bring bad luck to both of them. All things considered, they really had to watch their steps in those days (—pun intended).

One thing is for sure—all these magic formulae are aimed at two targets, insuring a lasting affection and warding off any evils that might threaten wedded bliss. But believe Br'er Pat, it takes something a little more substantial than rice and veils to insure a Happy Marriage and it takes more than a circle around an imaginary vein to guarantee an "ever after" love.

The real magic begins when you buy your Happy Marriage Insurance policy even before you *meet* your future partner (directions to follow). Then both of you invest a great deal of yourselves in it *before* your wedding day, and be prepared to go on investing *after* the bride has been ferried over the threshold.

Now here's some simple, modern, dependable Marriage Magic for "getting off on the right foot."

Is It for Real?

Here's the $64,000 question. "If we're *truly* in love," says Wendy confidently. And parents, who've been there before, beg, *"Wait* and be *sure!"* I'm not selling young love short when I say that's sound advice. Honest! I went "steady" twice, for three weeks as a high school freshman, and for six months as a sophomore. I was "sure" each time. My heart did the cha-cha, my ears rang, my brain went into orbit—

each time. It was a painfully serious, and delightfully uncomfortable form of teen-time romance on both occasions,
but it wasn't the stuff marriages are made of.

How can you tell the difference?

The first rule is, *give it the Time-Test*. Get acquainted!
Does that sound silly? Well, it isn't. I haven't forgotten how
it goes—you meet someone and there's an atomic crash. Your
heart and your knees develop lives of their own and your
head gets full of pink cotton. Cupid's guided missile has
scored a direct hit. It *must* be True Love. But if you're hasty
you may find yourself quaking at the altar, like the bride
whose mother found her weeping bitterly just before her
wedding. "My dear," said her Mom, "this is no time to cry.
Why, the day I was married was the happiest day of my life."

"But that was different," sobbed the girl. "You married
Dad; I'm marrying a complete stranger!"

Don't let that happen to you. Sometimes when my pals
have wanted to dash lickety-split from the first kiss to the
church I wonder by what yardstick they can be so *sure*.
Maybe they believe in the magic of the Bachelor Button or
Daisy test. You know, one petal at a time now, Love-Friend-
ship-Courtship-Marriage—or the little blue flower the Orientals thought could tell a guy whether he'd found the right
girl. If he picked his bachelor button early in the morning,
didn't look at it for twenty-four hours, and it was still fresh
and "true blue" he was on the right beam (it helped to water
your lapel often). Silly as these sound, any other test except
the *Time-Test* is just as sappy. You've simply got to give
yourselves time to know each other! Let's admit you're at-
tracted, that you're filled with mutual admiration. In short,
that you're "in love." Granted. Will you believe me when I
tell you this isn't enough to last a lifetime? It can add up to
a charming romance—but it's the *plusses* that count on the
long pull from spring to summer, and then on to autumn
and winter. Don't be afraid to let time test the caliber of your

love. If it wilts in the summer, believe me, marriage wouldn't have kept it alive! Time's done you a favor.

There are 4 plusses which I think are necessary for Happy Marriage Insurance and only Time can reveal them. First, *attraction plus companionship.* A wise man has said: "It is not lack of love but lack of friendship that makes unhappy marriages." Chew that one awhile.

One of my cagiest buddies, George Hill, has finally gone and gotten himself engaged to a pretty, talented, popular gal —but no prettier, no more talented, no more popular than some of the other beauties he's been dating for years. When he told me he'd finally been "hooked" I asked, "How do you know for sure this is *it?*"

"Because," he said, "we have a ball together no matter what we're doing." He explained that he certainly found her physically attractive but admitted that he had felt that same kind of attraction in other girls and in the end it wasn't enough. They had nothing in common. "But as I really got to know Liz," he said. "Well, I just enjoy her company more than anyone else's in the world." The physical attraction was still there—but as time passed it ceased to be so important, and without this clouding his mind he was able to size her up more rationally.

Now, I buy this explanation because it was the same with Shirley and me. Sure, I thought she was (and is) the most attractive girl I know, *plus* the best company. Once when we quit going steady at my parents' request, because they felt we were getting too serious too soon, we both just wound up not dating at all. We were each in Nowheresville—alone. She was the only girl I really cared to be with—my favorite companion. We had a lot in common. We both liked sports, liked singing, movies, laughed at the same things—and it didn't matter where we went. I enjoyed taking her to church or bringing her home just as much as taking her to a party or a show.

Second, there's *admiration plus trust*. This means more than simply trusting someone not to flirt or mess around. That's understood, and required, of course. But there's another kind of trust where your admiration is constant at all times and in all places. You trust your girl or your fella not to let you down, to be the same in any situation or with any people. If you only enjoy someone at a party, or with his crowd, or out under the moon, but don't look forward to being with him in church or sitting around your folks' living room, there's something missing. Something important.

Take a little more time. Take a *lot* more time. These things don't enter so strongly into courtship—but they're a *vital* part of marriage. A real sexy dresser might be a big hit with the gang, but you'd be surprised how self-conscious it can make you if she happens to be your wife. The life of the party, the boy with the jokes, the flashy clothes, looks very different when you're married to him, and he *isn't* always the life of the party around the house.

If your family and friends, as they have time really to get acquainted with your True Love, honestly don't care for him, please take a whole *lot* more time. It's true you're the one who has to live with him—but "ever after" can be a long lonely time if you're cut off from your own folks; and besides, sometimes they, with their unclouded minds, these people who genuinely want you to be happy, can see things at once that only time will reveal to you. They might even be right—once in a while!

Third, comes *love plus liking*.

It's easy to love and live with someone's virtues. It's a different thing to continue to love her and live with her faults. An important part of judging True Love is being realistic about these faults. Everybody has them (even you) and certainly love will make a guy or gal *try* to improve, but don't expect miracles. The spots may dim, but the leopard remains a leopard and what was a "cute little trick" in the springtime of romance (I remember one guy whose fiancee talked Baby

Talk—yeah!) may be neither cute nor little come summer or autumn.

You take my revoltin' habit of being late. Go on—take it, please! I think that if I could ever be on time everywhere, Shirley and I would have a lot fewer hassles. Recently she told me that in high school she knew about this and didn't mind much. It was "cute and interesting, a part of my personality." It tickled her when I'd pick her up late, cram her into the car and say, "Watch out. You'll sit on my dinner." There on the front seat would be a plate of food I hadn't had time to eat at home. She'd laugh and maybe feed me on the way to the movie, to save time.

But now, after goin' on seven years of marriage, when it's a dinner *she's* cooked and watched get cold, she doesn't laugh so much. Wonder why?

Now, I try and I try. I'm forever saying, "all right, you'll remember this day because it's the last time I'm *ever* gonna be late"—but somehow I just can't catch up with the clock. Shirley has finally, and wearily, decided that I just lack organizational ability—plan too much and underestimate the time necessary to accomplish—and somehow she's managed to adjust somewhat, just as I've managed to improve—somewhat. But believe me, she doesn't think it's cute or laughable. And it isn't easy on her, poor gal.

So take it from me—or if not from me from Shirley—it's important that you *like* your True Love and are going to be willing and able to adjust to his or her faults.

The fourth test is that, as time goes by, *what pleases her (or him) pleases you.* This means more than just having mutual interests. It means we've learned to love someone else more than we love us, remember?—and until that happens, love is pretty shallow, really only self-love reflected back to us as the admiration in another's eyes. We're really saying, "I love you because you love *me*—and want to please *me*." The obvious danger here is if we spot a little more admiration in a new pair of eyes we may love *them*. But when we can say, and mean, "*I* am really happiest when *you* are happy. I love *you* and am going to honor, cherish, and protect *you* no matter what happens to *me*," then when all the early petals fall off our spring romance, and we're faced with budgets and dishes and diapers (and this time comes, ol' friend!) there'll still be sound fruit on the branches. There'll be apples on your tree even in winter—if you have to tie them there yourself!

This kind of love brings *lasting* magic, not the hasty Houdini type. If you can pass the Time Test you've got the right foot forward. Now, when do you take the all-important step?

Are We Old Enough to Marry?

I, personally, don't think the answer to this is a matter of age. I've known couples who were "old enough" at nineteen (Shirley and Pat Boone, natch!) and others who didn't seem old enough at twenty-nine (names censored!). The real question is, are you *mature* enough to take the responsibility? And maturity is simply "a state of *full* development." Here's where you can begin investing in Happy Marriage Insurance even before you meet your One-And-Only.

Let's face facts. Accordin' to available statistics, one divorce is granted in the United States for *every four* marriage licenses issued! I don't like to call this sorry condition to your attention, but you see it and many of you suffer from it. This is a point you've written to say I ignored in other talks, and I know from what you write that you don't want to become that tragic one-in-four that signifies failure and heartbreak. How can you avoid it, since "just love" isn't enough?

A White House conference on family life some years ago reported: "The alleged grounds for divorce are merely pegs upon which the decree is hung. *The real grounds lie in the character defects of one or both spouses.*"

This has nothing to do with age. Character defects are just symptoms of immaturity—a refusal to develop.

A boy and girl actually came to see me in New York not long ago to discuss the problem: should they marry? or should they wait? Both were nineteen. Both were sophomores in college and had jobs at the same time. They'd been dating for over two years, were sure it was for real, and considered themselves engaged. Both families were happy about the proposed marriage, but wondered if marrying while in college would eventually keep them from finishing school.

As I listened to these two young lovers I remembered the questions Shirley and I had had to ask ourselves before we faced a minister to take our vows. Did we see our responsibilities clearly? Could we fulfill them? Could I work, support a wife, and still get a diploma? Would marriage interfere with my grades?

Those are some tall question marks, brother. When we figured we had all the right answers, we eloped to Springfield, Tenn., and were really on our own—for good!

On that last question (about grades) I could give the young couple the answer as it worked out for me, and they could carry it home to their parents who had encouraged them to come East for our talk. Marriage had given me a greater sense of responsibility and incentive to do well. This objection answered, I advised them to go ahead and get married if they really wanted to. Why? Because it had worked for Shirley and me? No. Because, as far as I could tell, they were mature people.

Their aims and principles checked out, and the chief problems Shirley and I faced in the young-married-and-going-to-college days—they seemed to have well in hand. Both had jobs. She had a car bought and paid for by herself. He had a savings account he had been accumulating. Both were determined to finish college. They spent all their spare time together anyway—and here they stood to gain, because once Shirley and I were married, spending time together wasn't as difficult and didn't have to be stolen from jobs and studies.

To my mind, these two were old enough to get married. They were ready, mature, and responsible. They could be completely independent of their parents (if you gotta mooch, don't marry!). If you want to know whether you, personally, are mature enough, or whether you are making good progress in that direction, ask yourself these questions:

How close am I to taking full charge of my own life and conduct? Have I developed *self*-reliance? *Self*-control? *Self*-discipline? Or am I still dependent on everyone around to do things for me? Does someone have to remind me to pick up my clothes, do my home-work, straighten up my room, get there on time? (Ouch!)

Have I made (or am I making) myself a desirable mate? Do I guard my conduct and reputation? Have I developed the skills necessary for my part in marriage? (Financial responsibility and such for boys—household skills for girls.) Have I gained a proper understanding of sex *from a trustworthy source* (parents, or ministers or doctors recommended) and abstained from cheap experiments or gossip?

Do my family, teachers, and friends trust me willingly with responsibility? Has anyone ever said: "If you want it done, get Jane—or Joe—to do it?" If so, is your name Jane or Joe?

Am I resourceful? Do I keep my head and know what to do in an emergency even if I'm alone? Am I in constant need of entertainment, or can I find plenty to do if left to myself for a while?

Those are for you alone—but here are a few to be faced by the engaged couple as a team: *Can we solve our differences of opinion by compromise?* This doesn't mean "you take, I give"—or vice versa. It literally means both yielding a little here and there. Here's an example. Shirley didn't want me to have a sports car. To her it meant high speed and low safety. I wanted very much to have a sports car but I didn't want my wife to get an ulcer every time I drove out of the garage (can't stand a burping wife!). So we compromised. Shirley agreed to the sports car—and I agreed to have a governor put on it so it wouldn't go over sixty. Fair enough? (Later on she developed confidence in my self-government, and the governor was removed.)

And then there are *aims* and *goals,* those little items Wendy brushed over so lightly. But unless you ask yourselves: *Do we agree on vital issues?*—no amount of True Love can make two opposed ideals into one United Marriage. Oil and Water don't mix.

Take the issue of *Family Life.* Shirley's and my ideals were identical. A sizable family. A happy home. To try to live as nearly Christian lives as we could. A simple existence centered around God, our children, our work, and each other. Now supposing Shirley (or I) had wanted instead, a penthouse, Page 30 in Who's Who, and maybe (ghastly thought!) poodles instead of children. We'd have had a pretty rough time making one set of aims and ideals blend with the other, right? Other vital issues definitely include *Religion* (not to mention politics), and *money matters* (try contributing liberally to the church *and* your Uncle Sammy if you and your spouse don't have an understanding).

Turning to the experts we find Superior Court Judge Roger Alton Pfaff, who presides over the Conciliation Court of Los Angeles County, one of the few courts in the country that specializes in trying to put the Magic back into marriage after a divorce has been asked for. A tough trick in any state!

Judge Pfaff agrees with the goin' statistics that a teen-age marriage has *fifty per cent less chance* of surviving than any other. "The difficulty is that, in the late teens, these young people are usually making two of the most important decisions of their lives when they are least prepared to make them—the choice of a mate, and the choice of a vocation." Why are teen-agers unprepared? "Lack of maturity," says

Judge Pfaff— (or lack of "a full state of development plus Common Sense").

Here, according to the Judge and Meyer Elkin, the Court's supervising counselor, are the Six Danger Zones for young couples. You can easily check yourself on whether you are apt to be in any one of them:

1) *Immaturity.* You can't get married until you're grown-up. Everybody knows that, so, in a sense this covers almost everything else. Very few of us are completely adult at any age but the teen-agers who are thoroughly responsible (mature) people *in the marrying sense* are as rare as white crows. Can *you* fly and say "Caw?"

2) *In-laws.* The problem of a husband (with a scorched shirt) or a young wife (with hurt feelings) running home for help can really slice up a young marriage. Affectionate, loving, devoted to your parents, you should be! But not dependents, either emotionally or financially. Mr. Elkin declares flatly that experience shows *no couple should ever move in with the parents of either one.* Even if it's cozy and friendly it stunts maturity growth.

3) *Single friends.* These pose a real threat to teen-age marriage success that's often not recognized until too late. The safest course is to have friends among other young married couples. The single girl friend pulls the young wife away from responsibilities, tugs at her to adopt a less responsible frame of mind and activity. The husband's friends may still be hot-rodders. Or rudderless goof-offs. A young breadwinner can rarely afford the luxury of goofing-off. But the difficulty of teen-age couples breaking away and making a new social life altogether is tremendous.

4) *Arrival of the first baby.* At this point the "young couple" become "parents." What else? But most young people have had no preparation for this important event and the youngun which should be the greatest bond to hold them together, serves instead as a wedge to drive them apart. The husband may feel neglected because his wife is giving atten-

tion to the baby that she always gave to him. She, on the other hand, may feel that she's tied down, over-worked, and missing all the good times she used to have.

5) Lack of *"Get along skills."* Too many teen-agers starting with "nothing but love" are faced with not much know-how. The husband doesn't know how to make a living. The wife doesn't know how to run a house. They neither know how to manage money, if they *had* any. If this is the case you can see they're not mature enough to set up on their own. They still need dad to make the living, mom to run the house, and a weekly allowance.

6) *Religious Differences.* A marriage between two people of differing faiths puts a real strain on both of them as time goes by. The tension increases when children arrive and the question of religious training arises. Oh, you may have "settled it" before, but now that the children are *here,* it's different. Harmony is disrupted and sometimes devout relatives on both sides can make matters worse.

"Don't marry," warns the expert, "until you are sure you can deal with these successfully."

Judge Pfaff also lists in order, from his own experience, these six complaints and character defects as "the most common" termites that can very early begin to nibble away the foundations of a sound marriage. Now check yourself (*and* your prospective partner if you think you've found one) and see how you stand— Remember, you're never too young to start on this check list and become the sort of person who'll make an ideal liftime partner!

After 3 years of marriage husband complains of:	After 3 years of marriage wife complains of:
Problems of Communication:	*Problems of Communication:*
(Wife afraid or unable to talk things over. Harbors grudges, sulks, suffers in silence until . . . !)	(Thinks of nothing but business, hasn't time to talk over home problems, never says "I love you" anymore.)

Money Management:

(Extravagance. Not putting first things first, irresponsible, wants more than he can give her, unreasonable in demands.)

Money Management:

(Too little to spend, tightwad, spendthrift, doesn't bring pay home.)

Negative Self-Image:

(This is the emotional pattern of immaturity called lack of self-confidence. It shows up as irresponsibility, jealousy, possessiveness, intolerance, lack of initiative, waiting to be told to do things, aggressiveness, being bossy, loud, dependency, the complete clinging vine, feelings of inferiority and insecurity.)

Negative Self-Image:

(Same as husband.)

In-Law Problems:

(Wife runs to mamma or papa. Won't let them stand on own feet. Seeks sympathy and then quotes criticism.)

Conflict Over Children:

(Training, discipline, outside interests and friends, he disrupts her routine with kids constantly.)

Selfishness:

(I love *me* and I'm going to take care of *me* first!)

Selfishness:

("Get out in that kitchen and rattle those pots and pans. . . . You get me some supper, 'cause I'm a hungry man! Shake, rattle, and roll!")

Nagging:	*Third Person:*
(Wow! "Yakkety-yak and don't talk back!")	(Flirting, having to continue to attempt new conquests, and infidelity are listed by the experts as forms of immaturity.)

And here, as a further check for you older ones, is a portion of the E. W. Burgess and L. S. Cottrell marital adjustment scale as modified by P. Boone for engaged or steady-going teen-agers:

Are You Meant for Each Other?

(How well adjusted are you?)

1. If you had it to do over again, would you become engaged to (go steady with) the same person (15 points)
   a different person (1 point)
   no one (0 points)
2. How many things annoy and dissatisfy you about your fiancée and engagement (steady)? None (10 points)
   One (7 points)
   Two (1 point)
   Three or more (0 points)
3. Have you ever wished you had *not* become engaged (decided to go steady)? Frequently (0 points)
   Occasionally (2 points)
   Rarely (4 points)
   Never (15 points)
4. When disagreements have arisen they usually have resulted in fiancée (steady) giving in? (3 points)
   agreement by mutual give and take (10 points)
   neither giving in (0 points)

5. In leisure time both of the engaged pair (steadies) prefer
   to be "on the go" (3 points)
   both prefer to stay at home (10 points)
   one prefers to be "on the go" while the other stays
   home (0 points)

6. Do engaged pair (steadies) participate in outside interests
   together? All of them (10 points)
   Some of them (10 points)
   Very few of them (1 point)
   None of them (0 points)

7. Do you show affection to your fiancee (steady)
   every day? (10 points)
   occasionally (1 point)
   almost never (0 points)

8. (see opposite page)

Maximum score: 170 (Chances are that you're well adjusted).

If your score is 170-140 your adjustment is GOOD.

If your score is 139-105 your adjustment is FAIR.

If your score is below 105—CALL IT OFF!

If and when you check out on these you are probably "old enough" to get married. Have a lovely wedding (from $5 on up)—and when you're in your new home you can begin to build the "ever after" on a solid foundation.

Post Altar Marriage Insurance:

Here are a few Boone baubles for warding off the Evil Eye. *Don't drift away from small attentions.* Don't fall into the trap of putting off doing things for the one you love and doing for others instead, thinking that she'll understand. I'm guilty, but Shirley has a wonderful knack of doing the little things I ask her to do *right now*. If I mention that my vitamins need refilling or my hair brush needs washing, it's done the same day. It's not only that she finds time to fit it into her very busy schedule that touches me. It's the knowledge that she *thinks of me.*

8.

Check one on each item below	Always agree (10 pts)	Almost always agree (8 pts)	Occasionally disagree (6 pts)	Frequently disagree (4 pts)	Almost always disagree (2 pts)	Always disagree (pointy-head)
1—Conventionality (right, good and proper behavior)						
2—Philosophy of life (aims, goals and things believed to be important)						
3—Friends						
4—Dealing with adults (prospective in-laws)						
5—Ideals (code regarding love, play, religion, etc.)						
6—Handling finances						
7—Demonstration of affection						
8—Recreation						
9—Amount of time spent together						

And then we have a secret "small attention" that has meant a lot in our marriage. I have Shirley's permission to share it now, in case it helps someone else over the rough spots. From time to time I send my wife one single long-stemmed red rose —just that—no note—nothing more. But it pleases her more than a bouquet. It's often after we've had a hassle and it means: "The *one of us* is more important than all this fuss."

Second: *Marriage is no time to stop developing interests in common.* It's an opportunity instead to grow together along new lines. Not long ago, Jack Spina, my co-manager, invited us to a hockey game. Shirley had never seen one and didn't much want to, but she did want to spend the evening with Jack and me. The result? The Boones are hockey-happy! And I, well, I've learned to go shopping with Shirley, but I'm afraid Elvis will be bald before I develop a liking for it.

Third: and this I pass on to you from Mack Craig, the man I once told you of—my high school principal and chief non-family teen-age advisor, still one of my best friends. Mack said: *"If you and your wife can laugh together, see some humor in every situation, there's no problem you can't lick."*

Take a "situation" that developed recently. On our Chevy show I got soundly smooched, without any warning, by a Hollywood glamor girl with an accent and an enormous collection of jewelry (her first name is Zsa). Right on TV— you may have seen it! While I wiped the blush off, I ad-libbed, "Looks like I'll spend the night at the Athletic Club." But when I drove up in front of our house an hour later, it appeared to be no joke. No light was burning in any window. No little woman to greet me. As I opened the door I saw the TV still flickering in the den and decided Shirley had flounced off to bed without even bothering to turn it off.

How wrong I was! There, in the dim light, draped before the flickering screen, in jeweled slippers. a Chinese kimono, false eyelashes, and sporting every bit of jewelry she or the girls in the neighborhood own, was Shirley. Slowly she smiled, dropped the lashes, and said in a deep, accented voice, "Dahling, I've been vaiting for you!"

That's one side of it. But I saw Mack Craig and his wife Dottie prove that laughter has a deeper meaning, too, that it can soften the heartbreaks that inevitably must be faced at some point in married life. For last fall Dottie Craig died of cancer. She knew the truth some months before the end and the rest of us had known for a year. And right up to the last Dottie Craig smiled and laughed. She laughed at the inconveniences, at the fact that she couldn't do the things she once did, said she was getting fat and lazy just lying in bed. She made jokes as operations whittled away at her body, and her laughter fed Mack's soul. Though it broke your heart to see, she was magnificently gallant right up to the moment of parting as her brave good humor made it all bearable for the husband, family, and friends she loved.

The last, the best, the surest, way to ensure a Happy Marriage is to take God into your partnership. This, good friend, is the ingredient that gave Dottie her courage, and that brings grace and truth to every couple. He's a silent partner, true—but we've found Him the best. Whether your wedding is large or small, whether you elope or have twenty bridesmaids, don't trust to *luck* in this greatest adventure open to a young man and woman. Trust your Heavenly Father. Enter into Holy Matrimony asking His help, guidance, and support every step of the way. That's *real* marriage magic. Remember that "the family that prays together, stays together" and prayer shouldn't be limited to grace before meals!

Here's more evidence of the truth of that statement. A recent poll taken by Judge Pfaff showed that the most important factors in keeping a family together are: *Having an active religious affiliation* (goin' to church regular!), *having children,* and *owning a home*—in that order. One, two, three.

Judge Pfaff says, "My studies show that among ninety-five

per cent of the couples coming for divorces, either one or both of them do not attend church regularly. The reason seems clear. Those who do are maintaining orderly, stable lives, getting constant counseling from their church in one form or another, and *even the newly married church-goers have a more mature perspective on marriage and concept of the home than couples with many years duration where there has been no religious background."* See how faith and maturity go together?

Teen-agers who are church-goers right now are building toward a solid marriage—and, once married, it's the church-going family that prays—and stays—together.

So make your marriage a sacred thing and, if you fulfill your part of the bargain, God will fulfill His. That's why I still think the best wish we can give a bride and groom is the old, old one our great-grandmothers embroidered on samplers. "God Bless This Happy Home." And Shirley and I, when your time comes, from the bottom of our hearts wish the same to you!

8

The Whole World Challenges **You!**

Ever heard of a Doom-Peddler?

What do you figger one to be?

Well, it's what I'm not. It's the reverse of an Optimist and you'll remember, I'm an Optimist—a Hope Addict. I have a strong hunch that you teen-agers of today are the shining hope of the world, and I've already told you that from what I've seen of you the future looks safe to me.

However, as you've gotten older, you've probably found as I have that there's a *but* or an *if* tacked onto almost every positive statement. "Harriet will make a fine wife," says Mom positively, and then, raising her eyebrow, adds, "*if* she learns to cook," Or, "Gordon will graduate *magna cum laude—but* he'll have to bear down on his science." Or, your chum gloats, "My folks say I can have a horse," and then as an after-thought, "*if* I can pay for its keep *but* I can't seem to earn enough money."

You get the idea?

Well, I *do* think you are the hope of the world—*but* and *if!*

No, I'm not a Doom-Peddler. I have perfect faith in you

if you know what you're up against *but* we'd better start off
by admitting something. You young Jacks and Jills are going up the hill to assume control of a Very Serious Situation.
A pail of Hydrogen, as it were.

I know that's not news to you. I know too, that I'm not an
historian, a statesman, a sociologist. I'm not even your minister, teacher, or parent, and so I have no right to lecture or
preach. But I've read, studied and thought a big heap about
this world situation and how it affects you. I've traveled to a
lot of places; seen a lot of things; had a chance to ask a lot of
questions of brilliant, informed men and listened carefully
to their answers and I'd be from Coward City if I fell for the
temptation (and it's a very strong one) to spend these last
few chapters we have together making with the jokes and
passing the bon-bons and pouring one more Coke for the
road, and all that jazz, instead of discussing this Serious Situation with you.

Good showmanship says, if you want an audience to love
you "always leave them laughing when you say goodbye."
But for now, I'm not a showman. I'm your friend. And I'd be
less than a friend if I didn't warn you that the world today is
no joke!

You can laugh as you meet the challenges. You'd do that
anyhow. It's the All-American way for meeting things head-
on. And it's the victorious way. But we've got to get serious
while we try to blow away the confusion by (first) a clear,
definite statement of what the real issues are; and (second)
by facing as honestly as possible that earnest question of
yours, "What can *I* do about them?"

Walter Lippmann wrote not long ago: "The voices that
will serve this country, and indeed save it, will be those of
stern men demanding hard things." Doesn't sound like a
popular showman type, does he? Sounds more like today's
football coaches.

Now, I don't qualify as a stern man or a football coach, but

I'd be a cream-puff if I didn't tell you that while there's plenty you can do, starting today, it's not gonna be easy. It wasn't easy for the men and women who started this big country ticking, and it won't be for you who keep it running. And tomorrow, when you're running the whole show, when you're the voters, parents, teachers, scientists, executives, government officials—well, you're going to have a ball *if* you're ready for the responsibility *but* you'd better get in training *now*. As for you pretty gals, you not only have to be ready to play any on-stage role these days from senator to scientist *but* you have to stand responsible for inspiring the men and preparing the *next* generation—your children. So these challenges are doubly important to you. If you never drop the role of Housewife, remember, behind every great man has been a great woman, a wife or mother. Honest Abe said that, and it's still true.

Now, please forgive me if I get kind of excited and carried away in the next few pages. I'll try to keep things conversational, but I still hope you'll feel the urgency of what I have to say. I've never talked or written to you about *anything* more important than what's coming up!!

The clearest statement I've heard of what you face came from J. Edward Murray, managing editor of the Los Angeles *Mirror-News*. It may have been stated more profoundly somewhere else—I don't know. Ed Murray doesn't claim it's an exclusive, only that "the important role of an editor and his newspaper . . . is to tell readers what they are up against" in language they can understand, and I think he did exactly that for *you* when he publicly issued four "Challenges to Youth, 1960."

So with Mr. Murray's permission, I'm latching on to his basic statement of these Four Challenges—together with some side trips, explanations and observations I've dreamed up on my own or collected elsewhere—to get the message across. I sure hope it works.

Challenges to Youth, 1960's:

The first challenge is—peaceful competition with the Russians!

The second challenge is—making democracy work in a wealthy society!

The third challenge is—avoiding nuclear war!

The fourth challenge is—the challenge of each man to think as clearly as he can and choose the right course of action, the highest value, for himself! Naturally, this applies to girls, too.

Please, PLEASE look these four statements over carefully! You can throw this book away then, if you want to. You may be afraid of topics like these . . . I hope not. We'll talk about each one separately, and I'll do my dagnabbest to make it all interesting. *I pray to God that I can,* because I know you're not likely to stick with me through a lot of dull lecturing, no matter how good friends we are!

But brother . . . and sister . . . if I, or Ed Murray, or *somebody,* can't interest you in these challenges, the whole free world is gonna go right down the drain! And you—and your children—may live in the Communist United States!

It's that serious.

**The Future Challenge Is Peaceful
Competition with the Russians.**

This, says Ed Murray, "has the old-fashioned clarity of the duel. We must win, and stay ahead, or die, because the competing totalitarian communist system openly threatens to 'bury us' if it can."

Now that stated challenge is pretty clear, and obviously it's no joke. Nobody's laughing, brother. We might as well face another fact. The two opposing systems, our Four Freedoms against their totalitarianism (that, by the way, is the system where the state is boss—completely), *do not play by the same rules* and are diametrically opposite to one another (which simply means 'never the twain can meet').

To get back for a minute to oyster opening as an example (remember Chapter 3?). We agreed that teen-agers in America live by the old proverb, "The World Is My Oyster," and potentially this is true. But it's *not* true over in Russia under the present communist system because communism says you haven't *got* an oyster! *All* oysters, along with any pearls they contain, belong to the state!

The "men on the street" in Russia are in much the same position as the two fellows walking along the beach at low tide, who saw an oyster. Both stooped to pick it up, both worked to open it, and a dispute ensued as to which man had the right to its content. A government official, passing by, was called to settle the dispute. As each finished telling his story, the newcomer quietly pocketed a couple of pearls and gravely ate the oyster. Then he handed each a shell. "I award you each a shell," he smirked happily. "The oyster belongs to the state!"

Remember this, and remember it well: it is only under a free system of government that each man has the right to find his own oyster, the right to open it, the right to claim his own pearls, and the right to appeal his differences before a bar of justice. And justice itself is a precious pearl.

But we're fooling ourselves if we believe that an unhappy Soviet people are momentarily on the verge of "throwing off the yoke of Communism." The fact is—they're quite proud of the advances they've made! To understand this we have to remember something. We were *born under a free system.* Our parents and probably grandparents and maybe even great-grandparents and so on, were born free. Not so with the Russian. Today, the average Russian thinks he's doing great. Before 1917, in the days of the Tsars, most of them never even saw an oyster, let alone were handed the shell. Their present system, they believe, is working for them. Why not?

They're getting more and better housing, more and better stuff to eat and wear than five or ten years ago, and, since they have been purposely fed an entire misconception of our system, it isn't easy for us to show them that there's a still better way.

Besides, as their leaders are quick to point out to them, the Russian system has brought them to the point where they are able seriously to challenge *us,* America the Bountiful, America the Mighty, America for whose accomplishments they have always had a large admiration.

So, in this specific challenge, we must either get enthusiastically behind our own way of life and prove that we can meet and better any peaceful competition—OR see *them* convince *their* people and the rest of the world that *theirs* is the winning system, that ours is old-fashioned and inadequate. And if this happens, we will be "buried" indeed!

A real life drama enacted early this year in a Senior High School in New Brunswick, New Jersey, made a deep impression on me. You may have read about it. A social studies teacher, Ewing McKown, suddenly announced to a class of thirty seniors, "The state is supreme."

"People over sixty-five must be exterminated for the good of the state."

"Anyone defending democracy in this class will be punished. . . ."

"A dictatorship is the best political system, and the individual is only an insignificant cog in the state machine. . . ."

The twenty-eight-year-old teacher allowed no one to smile, to talk, to cross his legs, in the classroom. They stood at attention to recite, and if any student differed in opinion with Mr. McKown, they had to copy, word for word, editorial opinions from the local papers.

Now, this twenty-eight-year-old teacher hadn't tapped out mentally. "I was searching for some way to make totalitarianism come alive, to show some of its harshness," he explained. And so, when the class voted its approval, they began a live experiment—totalitarianism practices and propaganda in an American classroom. But at the end of two weeks, the class was in an uproar. Using the "informer" and "traitor" methods, the teacher set up a realistic spy system and eventually one girl, according to Mr. McKown, began actually to believe her parents were informing on her. When Mr. McKown climaxed his performance by insisting that only one religion, a state religion, should be allowed, the volcano erupted!

But this teacher had done his job. First, he had taught thirty young Americans to value what they had formerly taken for granted, and, as one seventeen-year-old said, "It taught me how very little I really know about democracy."

Even if they don't use the ingenious tactics of Ewing McKown, our schools, our newspapers, magazines, and TV and radio commentators are trying to see that we know "a very great deal" about our form of government, its advantages, trials, decisions—not only because we've got the greatest, but because you've got to know about it. You're *it!* It's *you!*

So, let's get out our flags and wave 'em!

Let's be "Early Americans" and change that nickname of "Ugly Americans" that we've been given because of a small touch of laziness and a large touch of unawareness in the world competition.

Let's have a clear purpose.

David Sarnoff, in an article on our National Purpose, suggested that "Our message to humankind must be that America has decided irrevocably to *win* the 'cold war' and thereby cancel out the destructive power of Soviet-based communism."

This would seem to me to be a great slogan under which to unite to win the first challenge of "Peaceful Competition

with Russia." All we desire to defeat are "Destructive pow-
ers"—not nations or peoples, anywhere.

And once united, we will find what Abraham Lincoln said
a century ago, to be true: "Determine that the thing can and
shall be done, and then we shall find the way."

9

Mom and Dad Were Cream-Puffs

Hang on now! We're shifting into second gear—don't poop out on me!

The second main challenge, (remember Ed Murray's 4 challenges to youth?) is trickier than the first. So switch to oxygen and we'll blast off.

It's the Challenge of Making Democracy Work in a Wealthy Society.

What does that mean? This: we have freedom. And we're rich. Can we mix the two and make it work?

When your great-greats and my great-greats—like D. Boone—were all fired up with frontier spirit, their challenges were clear cut and real basic. They had to conquer a wilderness, provide food and shelter and clothes, build railroads and cities across a vast emptiness. There were two spark plugs that kept their engines running at top speed and their enthusiasm high. *First,* the challenge to raise up a standard of living that meant comfort for all and some luxuries for most.

That has been achieved. Never before in history have so

many lived so well, with so many opportunities. In other words, nobody ever had it so good! I, myself, counted fifteen TV antennas on the hogans of an "isolated" Indian village a couple of summers ago! Imagine those Indians sittin' there watching "Wagon Train!"

I read that in fifteen years the average United States teen-ager's pocket money has increased from $2.50 to $10.00 per week (doesn't include you? That's probably good.) ; that you teen-agers today, alone, represent a hefty nine and one-half *billion* dollars in purchasing power (roughly a third of which you earn at part-time work and summer jobs), and that you spend yearly to the tune of 145,000,000 *gallons* of ice cream, $9,000,000 in home permanents, $75,000,000 on records. Now that's livin' pretty high on the hog, as we say down Texas way. Starting right early, too!

The *second* spark plug that fired the frontier spirit in great-great grandpap's day was the desire *to make America great*.

And that too, has been achieved. America today is, as Werner von Braun said, "not only the richest and technically most advanced country in the world, but also the one whose people laugh and enjoy God's world more than anywhere else."

But now that these goals are fulfilled, the old challenges aren't there anymore to set us on fire.

This is "the terrible challenge of *no* challenge"—or, at least, no obvious challenge!

There are, it seems, more subtle dangers in having too much—than in having too little.

Are We Too Soft to Care?

The question was put to students at Pierce Junior College in Southern California this way: "Do you think the present generation is too materialistic?" Or, too "gone" on comfort? Sally Loeffler, a pretty co-ed, said, "Yes . . . it's a terrible thing to discover that we spend more time collecting, licking, pasting, and redeeming Blue Chip stamps than we do in prayer."

But another student came back, "I can't see anything wrong with my mother using an automatic washer rather than a bar of soap and a scrub board. So what's wrong with stereo, a nice car, a camera, a television set, nice clothes, and so on and so on?"

But Sally makes a good point. I'd say there's absolutely nothing wrong with stamp collecting or a nice TV (especially if you watch the Pat Boone Show), but it's a question of the order of their importance on your scale of values. You have to put God and prayer *ahead* of Blue Chip stamps, and your country ahead of any TV (including the Pat Boone Show). To have the true American pioneer spirit, you'd have to be willing cheerfully and immediately to sacrifice "both me and TV," if it would help America.

We'll agree that if you and I and our neighbors can keep the spirit of the "Early Americans," Uncle Sam can't be weakened by those modern viruses of indifference and materialism. (Now, here again are the *"if's"* and *"but's"* that follow this positive statement.)

But those viruses have attacked us—because we don't have a clear-cut purpose that would "immunize" us against them. Remember, when you quit growing, you start dying! You can't stand still . . . and when we stop marching toward a worthwhile goal, we start sinking in the quicksand of self-interest, and those virus-bugs of indifference and materialism will swarm all over us!

So you have the problem, *worse* than your parents did, of being strong in *spite* of soft living and many luxuries! If you fail, if you get soft, your children of the future will be even softer than you! Get the picture?

But *If* you, a teen-ager who *could* sit back and take it easy; who *could* "let George do it," while you bought another 145,000,000 gallons of ice cream; who *could* have life softer than mom's and dad's—if you face up to this challenge, you may find your life a little harder than your parents did (in fact, you'll make 'em look like "cream-puffs"!),—*but* you can reach heights that weren't open to them.

And you'll *keep* America great!

Juvenile Delinquency:

Our Uncle Sam, weakened by the viruses of indifference and materialism, has caught two terrible *diseases!* One is J.D.

Do you remember those questions we talked about in the introduction (I sneaked one in on you, didn't I?) that were asked of me by some high school newspaper editors and reporters? *"To what do I attribute juvenile delinquency? Is the punishment severe enough for the offenses? Would a curfew law help?*

Well, hang on, here's where I try to answer 'em!

To what, in a few hundred words, do I attribute juvenile delinquency?

Well, in big cities where folks of different backgrounds are all jammed together without proper recreational facilities, there seems to be a kind of volcanic reaction. Teen-agers who "don't know what to do with themselves" erupt and the resulting fireworks aren't pretty.

The movies and TV and even the newspapers and magazines publicize and sometimes glamorize these symptoms and that's no help, either.

Anyway, that's one cause of J.D. Crowded, underprivileged areas. Here's another.

Having too much is sometimes worse than having too little! Somehow, the family that doesn't have to worry about meat-and-potatoes often forgets about working, playing and praying *together*. They don't share problems or very much love. They're too busy having fun, joining clubs, giving parties and keeping up with the Joneses. As a result, the teenager looks for companionship and a sense of belonging elsewhere—and so the "gang' is formed.

But if you put this all together I think you can see a common cause. *The juvenile delinquent's real challenges in life have not been made clear to him for one reason or another, and his energies are being wasted on foul play.*

As for curfew laws and punishments—sure, a curfew would help if the kid you chased off the street has a happy, fun home to go to!

Now, I, personally, think as far as punishment is concerned, that it should fit the crime. If a young person is old enough to think out and commit a crime, he's old enough to suffer the consequences.

It's been my experience that most teen-agers know right from wrong—black from white—and won't call it gray; that a just, immediate punishment gains a teen-ager's respect where a wishy-washy attitude breeds contempt. Stay tuned— I'll illustrate.

Now, is there anything that you, personally, can do about this particular disease which attacks a small percentage of your number? I think so. I know of some startling cases where you've *already* done something. And I think it ties in with the other question you young newspapermen and women asked me: *"Considering the headlines about teen-age violence caused by about three per cent of the teen-agers, how can the rest of us counteract the bad publicity? How can we get newspapers to publicize the good side of teen-age activities?"*

Let's look at a couple of specific answers.

A number of years ago in Westwood, New Jersey, a teen-age boy read screaming headlines: "Juvenile killer caught . . . teen-ager shoots, kills, store owner in attempted robbery . . ."

That night he and five other high school chums held a council of war on his front porch. They decided that big *crime* by teen-agers made the news—so they'd try to make big news on the *good* side!

One of the girls, who wanted to be a nurse, remembered

that there was a desperate need for a hospital in their areas. "Let's raise enough money to build a hospital—that's big enough," she blurted out.

Now, here was a concrete challenge. A big *BIG* one.

The idea caught like wildfire. It captured the imagination not only of the so-called *good* teen-agers, but their rank increased to include many previous skeptics—athletes, school leaders in every field. And before they knew how it happened, they were enthusiastically joined by some of the "fringe delinquents," the pool room boys and bikini gals whose cynical attitude had been—"we belong to a delinquent generation"—and, "It's a crumby world . . . the big shots don't know what to do about it—what do they expect of us?" Big shots among street-corner gangs began to notice their ranks thinning as many of the kids hot-footed it over to where the new excitement was!

They discovered that the word "hospital" was a dud when it came to getting publicity—but "teen-agers" aroused a lot of interest. They organized spaghetti dinners, card parties, dances, cake sales, in different towns throughout the area. They handled a seventeen-thousand letter mailing for the adult Hospital Association.

At the end of the first year their results were tallied. $2,600 earned. Out of this sum the land for the hospital was purchased.

The papers picked this up—even the *New York Times!* Kids from other towns wrote to ask how they'd done it—and they spread the word.

The second year they found more money-making projects —like a booth at the North Jersey Kennel Club Dog Show (where they sold catalogues and shares on a portable radio— net $615). They conducted a census in the towns of Emerson, Hillsdale, and Westwood, for which a publishing house paid $700. They produced a skit at the local theater and three free concerts (with donations). The second year's net? $2,427.85. Two years' receipts: $5,027.85.

But the gain wasn't all in dollars. They hit their big objective—to make big news on the good side. And they also offered a clear, exciting challenge to some of their fellows who had been wasting their energies along some pretty "delinquent" avenues.

Makes you pretty proud, doesn't it? Me, too.

These are outstanding examples, sure. But you have the same kind of opportunities every day. In my senior year, as president of the student body at David Lipscomb Hi in Nashville, I participated in a program that won headlines for the young folk of *our* town. The Inter-Hi Student Council put on a big Fire Prevention Week, and I mean to tell ya that every radio station, newspaper, bus company, and even most ministers, helped us spread the good word about preventing People Roasts! By the end of the week, folks were scared to light a match! And all this was organized and executed by Teen-agers Only—and everybody knew it.

Since my time, the Inter-Hi group has put on Courtesy Week, Safety Week and I don't know what all. But the people of Nashville know pretty well by now what their young folks are made of! And the best part about things like this is that we remove the "creep-sign" from being *good*. We show the world what goodness really is—a vigorous, active, *happy* and *exciting* way of living. It requires all the courage, all the daring, and provides all the challenge that the so-called delinquent thinks he meets in gang life or in blind, dark alleys, or in cheap adventures.

For Pete's sake, let's get excited about goodness! It's never been tame! Or unexciting! Or for the wishy-washy feeble character! And I have a strong hunch that, if we, personally, would take the dare, we'd help by our example, not only ourselves and our country, but every delinquent that's looking for a clear challenge and an exciting direction for all his energies.

You can't do it? Neither can I. Not all the way. It's a big order. But we can try. We can do the best we can—and bet-

ter than we're doing now. And that, multiplied by 18,000,-
000 teen-agers, plus me, who still likes to play on your team,
would be enough to change more than just your publicity—
it could change the whole world!

Corruption:

Here comes the second disease that's attacked our wealthy,
virus-weakened Uncle Sam; some of it is sort of adult delinquency, but we'd better look anyway. There's public corruption, like fixed TV quizzes. Payola. False advertising. Union
gangsterism. Cheating in college. Income tax evasion.

Now, the worst of this stuff isn't that it happens. There've
always been cheaters and liars and gangsters coming out of
the woodwork. The real danger is that nowadays we say—
"so what?" We're used to it! And because somebody you
know does it, or, worse yet, "everybody does it," black suddenly becomes white. Or at least "gray."

Only it doesn't. It isn't. And you and I know it.

If a man wants to cheat, that's between him and his con-
science. But if he tries to kid himself that, "because everybody's doing it," it's really only a new way of refreshing the
memory (for a TV quiz) or a new form of Relative Mathe-
matics (for tax forms), he's got the virus bad! He's running
a fever that distorts all aims and challenges, weakens the will
and purpose, and can kill our way of life—because the "gray"
attitude is very contagious. And public corruption is a fatal
disease to a democracy.

Private corruption doesn't do it any good, either. Alcoholism, the use of narcotics, cheap sex for the sake of sex only,
speed thrills that cause highway disasters, crime, these have
been called the "rotten side of personal freedom" . . . in
other words, men can use freedom to destroy themselves if
they wish. The oyster goes bad, the pearls turn green, and
ptomaine poisoning sets in.

Here again, you teen-agers, with your sharp, lively sense

of justice, your clear vision of black and white, have been active already.

For example, on January 27, 1960, Leonard Moore, seventeen, a senior at Jordan High School in Long Beach, California, and his pal, Bob Murdock, also seventeen, and a senior at Lakewood High, were working at an all night drive-in dairy. Suddenly, two nineteen-year-old dope addicts, well "lit," burst in and leveled a gun and informed the stunned buddies, "This is a stick-up!" When Lenny hesitated a moment in getting the money, one of the hold-up boys shot.

Young Moore was dead-on-arrival at the emergency hospital.

Bob Murdock and three hundred other teen-agers attended the funeral. Then they formed SCAN—Student Crusaders Against Narcotics. Their objective? To strengthen California laws against dope pushers, the kind of pushers who had "hooked" the dead boy's killers and indirectly caused his murder.

They raised money through appeals on local radio stations and in newspapers. Then, in two buses provided by Tanner Gray Lines, using gasoline and oil donated by a major oil company, young Murdock and sixty-eight other youngsters descended on the state capital at Sacramento. They visited the governor, Edmund G. (Pat) Brown. And with the help of assemblyman Samuel Geddes of Napa, California, they saw almost every state senator and assemblyman.

Bob Murdock told the governor: "You and you alone can give us the weapon we need to defeat this state's number one problem. We petition you to call an immediate special session of the legislature to give police the laws they need to protect California."

While Governor Brown did not call the special session, he said, "I must admit I am surprised at the knowledge you young people have demonstrated on this subject. Because of the information that you and others have provided, I am

appointing a special commission to review our handling of
the entire narcotics menace. I am also instituting a seven-
point program that includes special attention to capturing
the 'big fish' who profit from pushing dope as well as to
improved policing of the Mexican border. . . ."

But SCAN didn't quit even then! They went on quietly
contacting high school students throughout the state. A "return assault" on the capital could be launched if promised
action didn't materialize. "A second time," said young Murdock, "we feel we could muster not sixty-nine, but *ten thousand teen-agers!* We're trying to show the grown-ups that
dope addiction does exist among some young people. If something isn't done, the moral and physical fiber of young America is being threatened . . ."

I told you I could prove that your generation wasn't
"spoiled" or "flabby"—and that you're ready to get in there
and *fight* for "the moral and physical fiber of young America," if the challenge is clear!

Look at what a group of teen-agers have done for themselves and their parents where the problem is alcoholism. In
1956, a group was formed in Pasadena, California, calling
themselves, "Alateens," and today they have similar groups
all over the United States. Alateens banded together "to help
teen-agers to understand and help the alcoholic parent" by
studying the principles of Alcoholics Anonymous.

I once attended an Alateen meeting with a young friend of
mine and it made a terrific impression on me. . . . These
kids were sharing their "strength and hope with each other
to solve a common problem."

Talk about discipline! And courage! And faith! The very
vital "goodness" here was electrifying.

Some of them I met were fortunate, because when they
came into Alateen, their "problem parent" was already a
member of AA and was a "non-practicing" alcoholic. Their
purpose then was to understand their parents and their new

way of life. Then they hoped to help them get stronger and stronger all the time. But many start with a "practicing" alcoholic in their home and their first question was "why?"

Clare, a newcomer, asked it: "Why does my mother have to drink and spoil everything?"

A boy we'll call Danny gave Clare her answer. Danny was fifteen and had come to the group only four months before. He'd been silent, sulky, and when he *did* talk, he stuttered.

Now he spoke right up.

"Uh-if you really love your mom and w-want to help her, you have to r-really try to understand that your mother is a sick person. It was a relief to me to find that out. I mean, I felt b-better to know that she didn't do it to *spite* me, any more than she'd get small-pox to spite me. All the AA's and the doctors s-say the same thing. So the 'why' is—that your mother has a disease. If you o-only believe that, you'll feel sorry for her and you can help her."

"People with small-pox don't hit you with a lamp," Clare protested. "They stay in bed and take medicine. It's easy to be nice to them. But what do you do when your 'sick' mother throws things?"

There was a pause. Danny obviously had to struggle with himself to go further. I found out later that it was the first time he'd ever talked about his problem at one of the meetings. "Well, m-my dad still d-drinks. B-but I think I've found a pretty good w-way to help him. See, he gets kind of m-mean when *he* drinks, too. Well, w-when I see trouble coming and I c-can't leave the house, I try to b-be very still, like a chair. I don't get mixed up in scenes any more. I d-don't argue with him, or t-try to blame him for anything. If he bawls me out, I just take it . . ." For a second there was silence. I saw tears in his eyes. ". . . a-and when he . . . h-hits me . . . I . . . uh, I just kind of act like I'm s-sorry I mean, sort of l-like I *deserved* it." Danny took a deep breath and went on. "And most important of all, the next d-day I just forget all about it. I don't fuss at him or anything. I t-try not to even let him t-think about it. I just try to uh-act normal no matter what happens."

He sat down. Clare, like all the rest of us, was obviously moved. In a minute, she asked the question I was told most all of them ask. "You say I can help my mother. If I do what you tell me to, will she quit?"

The senior member, a pretty seventeen-year-old gal named Donna, answered that one—and the answer was that they couldn't promise. "It will help you to live with her, and her to live with you. But we can't *guarantee* that she'll get well— only that she could! AA isn't for all the people who need it. It's for people who *want* it. Even God can't force answers on people against their desires.

"But it does help those of us with this problem who need to love and respect our parents so badly, and usually feel pretty much the opposite. It brings us to a place where we can begin to understand."

One of the older boys stood up and spoke, "A teen-ager doesn't bring an adult into AA. He certainly can't *make* his parent quit drinking. But the more information we have, the bigger the possibility that we can maybe show them a way. See, a change in attitude from even *one member of the family* can be contagious. The idea can spread from the teen-ager that the right attitude toward a sick person is to be help-ful rather than to condemn. If we can help our parents real-ize they're sick, I mean, not just morally weak, sometimes they start hoping and looking for the cure. Meanwhile, at least there's more harmony around the home. It's not easy. All of us know that. Sometimes you think you understand pretty well and then, all of a sudden, you get fed up. But we keep trying . . ."

And that's all any of us can do.

10

Who's a Chicken?

A pair of headlights slashed through the foggy night . . . at 90 miles an hour. They were attached to a souped-up '49 Chevy coupe, with fender-skirts, double exhaust, all that jazz. Inside, screaming with exhilaration and wildly cursing each other's clumsiness, four teen-age boys were playing "chicken."

It went this way. As the car hurtled along the highway, shrieking around the curves, often in the left lane, each boy took his turn at the wheel. Without any warning, the driver would twist around and lunge over into the back seat. His companion in the front then had to slide quickly under the wheel and floorboard the accelerator, while another boy clambered into the "ready" position in the front seat. For several minutes this frantic merry-go-round careened through the darkness. The first boy to touch the brake would be the "chicken."

Inevitably, like a reflection in the mirror, another set of headlights loomed ahead. Mickey tumbled over into the back seat, laughing hysterically, "Okay, Don baby! Take it—."

Don baby tried. He might have made it if he could've gotten under the wheel in time. But there *was* no more time—not for Don, Mickey, Al or Skip. Not for the Logan family returning from a movie in the other car. No more Time.

Just Eternity.

I can remember when a "chicken" was a small fat bird that laid eggs and grew drumsticks. But in the last several years "chicken" has become a bad word. It suggests cowardice and fear. To be a "chicken" is to lose face with the gang, to miss out on the fun . . . particularly in the Teen World.

I've done a lot of thinking about this chicken situation. I was lucky—I went to a school where the "crowd"—the majority—was interested only in good clean fun. The fellas who got into trouble, who broke the rules, who took the dangerous chances, were a small minority. It's probably true where you are . . . I hope so, anyway.

I'm not gonna talk about that minority. It doesn't take much brains to see the senselessness of risking your life or reputation in a stupid game like that. Oh, I took a few ridiculous chances in my teen years, usually with my buddy Billy Potter, but in ways that could've harmed only us, not others. We ran along ledges on top of buildings, clambered around on high bridges, swam out from shore much farther than we should have . . . always challenging each other. We were *nuts!*

But I want to talk about the majority of us—because we're almost all "chicken" about certain things. Like saying "no" to something we know's wrong (it takes more guts to say "not me" to the crowd than to go along). Like standing up and admitting we "goofed." Like trying to be a good influence on our friends—*leading* 'stead of following. In other words, *most* of us are real moral "chickens." I include myself.

In our sneaky introduction, I listed some questions I'd been asked by high-school journalists. This was one:

"Do you believe that our teen-age morals and ethical values have decreased and degenerated to some extent—and if they have, I want to know if rock-and-roll, the movies, the advertising world, the vicious literature (you can keep on going like that forever), is a determining factor in the deterioration of youth's moral values?"

I had to answer "yes" to both counts (*my* opinion). The way I see it, not just teen-age, but America's morals in general have slipped . . . *all* ages. It's part of this second big challenge of keeping America strong, now that our country's rich and successful.

Moral Ptomaine Poisoning:

We mentioned that the virus-bugs of Indifference and Materialism have weakened us. We've caught the rotten diseases of Juvenile Delinquency and Corruption. Well, there's something else that's weakening our moral body and feeding those diseases.

It's a steady diet of trashy, suggestive literature and violent, sexy movies and TV shows. Ed Murray called this *abuses of mass communication*. Dig? *And* a big hunk of this trash is aimed right at *you*—the teen-ager!

Look. You can't pour garbage into a well very long without contaminating the water. Can you? People gripe about rock-and-roll—I'm a lot more worried about the *movies* you see than the music you play! What's wrong with Rock and Roll? Why, it's just a sort of basic, simple excitement put to rhythm—or a solid loudness with a beat. That's all. Morally, it doesn't worry me, although when I listen to the swinging music of the 30's and the early 40's, to Tex Beneke, Glenn Miller, The Dorsey Boys, I wonder how we're gonna feel in ten years when we say to our ever lovin'—"Listen, dear, they're playing our song," and in the background we hear "Hound Dawg" or "Tutti Frutti"! We may feel short-changed then, but it's harmless now.

But . . . don't you feel a little guilty when somebody catches you looking at one of those fold-out pictures in the "men's" magazines? Don't you blush slightly when you're discovered reading "My Awful Confessions," or some mag like that? Don't you hesitate to mention that you saw "I Was A Teen-Age Sexpot" at the movies last night? I *hope* you hesitate, and blush, and feel guilty . . . if so, there's still hope for ya!

In these Do-It-Yourself days, you have to be your own garbage disposal unit. Your own censor. Here again, you'll have to be tougher than Mom and Dad, because they didn't have these weakening influences as they grew up. Oh, they had dirty pictures and books, but they were passed from hand to hand, not sold openly on the news stands! Sure, they had party movies in their day, but they were seen only at stag parties, not advertised in lights at the downtown theaters with "Adults Only" signs tacked on (which only serve as *invitations* to the teen-agers!

When I was 17, I sneaked downtown to see "Bitter Rice," with Silvano Mangano. It was an Italian movie with subtitles, and probably the most suggestive movie ever to hit Nashville. Every religious organization banned it, so naturally everybody went to see it. It was a rough movie, and 'though you couldn't understand the words, the actions and subtitles left *nothing* to the imagination.

I walked out of the theater a pretty aroused and frustrated young fella. For days I was hopelessly infatuated with beautiful Silvano Mangano. It was a very unhealthy thing, though, because the desires and dreams of this infatuation were naturally not good. How could they be, when they were inspired by a luscious actress, almost nude, in the wildest movie I'd ever seen?

Gradually I got over it, but my eyes had been opened too soon to a tough side of life. And now these movies surround us. We see the same thing in the newspapers, magazines and books.

How can you fight this trash?

Simple. Just don't take that change out of your pockets. Let the "men's" magazines, sordid confessionals, bloody comics and confidential gossip sheets gather dust on the news stands. They'll disappear in a hurry. Walk right on by theaters showing the Vile, Violent, Vice-orama pictures. The owners will get the idea pretty quick. Where TV is concerned, be like the young gal who read the previews of an upcoming show or movie . . . if it sounded pretty raw, she'd pull her dad off on the side and whisper, "Dad, I don't think Mom ought to see this kind of show!"

Y'see, publishers and producers and sponsors are putty in your hands. They only put out products they think you'll buy or pay to see! So far we've proved they're right.

But you can change that! However (here come those stern words again), it'll take some self-discipline, some courage with the "crowd," maybe even some popularity risks until the idea gets going.

Let's not kid each other (save that for the grown-ups). You *do* know black from white. You *do* know what's good clean fun and what's slightly tired vulgarity. And you *are* old enough to make these decisions for yourself.

This ties in with another question one of your reporters asked: *"Some time ago young people were trying to model themselves after outstanding men and women of this country. Now it seems that teen-agers are trying to model themselves after entertainers and movie stars. Do you think this is good or do you think teeners should strive after a more worthwhile goal?"* (Did he want Boone the entertainer or Boone the movie star to answer? Either way, I'm on the hot seat!)

I definitely *don't* think it's good for a huge flock of young folks to model themselves after entertainers or movie stars. (Me, or anyone else.) We've already decided it's very important for you to be—You! No one else! And certainly, the last thing this country needs to answer the Communist challenge is 18,000,000 Bogarts, Gables, Fabians, Monroes and Kookies! (I suspect we've got all the Boones we need, too.)

What happened to the days when Presidents, Generals, Doctors, Lawyers, Ministers and Writers were heroes? And what happened to the teen idols of radio and books who were real strong young Americans?

We kid about it some now, but I remember being pretty

sold on Jack Armstrong, the All-American boy; and Frank
Merriwell; and when I read *Dave Dawson at Annapolis,* wow,
did I want to be like him!

Listen, those books are still around. Look 'em up, will ya?
The man at the bookstore, or the local librarian, will not only
find those books for you, but he'll select others just as good!

It's swell to have heroes. You must develop ideals, but
make sure that you set your goals high! As my good buddy
Ira North says, "You'll never hit that bird way up yonder
in the top of the tree . . . unless you aim *high* enough!"

So be careful about what you read. Be careful about what
kind of movies you see. Check *TV Guide* to see whether the
TV show's worth your watching. If you don't, you're gonna
get morally and spiritually sick! Now, who's a "chicken?"

Let George Do It:

Here's another disease rich America has to fight!

Apathy is a good word for it. It's an "everybody complains
about the weather; nobody *does* anything about it" attitude.
We all complain about careless drivers, juvenile delinquency,
prejudice and a lot of other things. But the fact that very few
of us ever *do* anything about them is slowly killing America!
Once in a while, you hear of an exception.

Thomas Callahan, a student at Stagg High School in Stockton, California, was killed in an automobile accident with
another teen-age driver a couple of years ago. His fellow students decided to do something about it. With the help of the
Stockton College public relations class, the high school students conducted a poll among all teen-agers regarding teen-
age drivers and passed the results along as advice to parents:

First and most important, the teen-agers themselves listed:
"Don't let teen-agers have cars until they can buy them with
their own money."

Other recommendations for traffic safety which received
nation-wide attention:

Suspend first offender's license thirty days.

Learn where teen-agers get liquor and cut off the supply.
Enforce curfew laws.

Give each traffic violator a day in jail at hard labor. Now, here's a group that didn't wait to "let George do it!"

Remember, I said earlier that, if I had my way, we'd get all the parents in each age group together and insist that they agree on Basic Rules? Well, here's a bunch that really shoved ol' "George" aside—

Teen-agers in Albany County, New York, drew up their own *code of behavior* and agreed they'd all abide by it. The young folks first examined codes that'd been published in other parts of the country and decided what they'd accept for their own. Here are the rules they adopted:

1. All parties should be supervised. Supervision should be inconspicuous but available at all times.

2. The expected time of arrival and departure should be understood in advance by guests and their parents. The following are the recommended approximate hours for home-coming: Ages 12 to 14—11:00 P.M. . . . 14 to 16—midnight . . . 6 to 18—1 A.M. (The panel figgered this was generous.)

3. At the conclusion of a party, parents or hosts should be sure that arrangements are made for the safe transportation of guests, especially girls, to their homes.

4. Parents or hosts are urged not to admit uninvited guests. Party crashing should be discouraged at all times.

5. In general, parties should be limited to week-ends and vacation days.

6. Guests at a party should be careful not to damage furniture or other property. (Amen!)

7. Young people should be alert to the fact that when they drive someone in a car, they're responsible for that person's safety.

I didn't make those rules up. "George" didn't. The *kids* did!

Let's Be Like Everybody Else:

Our wealthy Uncle Sam has yet another bug to fight—
Conformity! A definition of conformity is "the un-thinking
imitation of current habits, good or bad." In other words, if
"everybody" does it, it's OK.

Occasionally, I'm asked to speak at church, just as I did
regularly for the Church of Christ at Slidell, Texas. (That's
right—Slidell. If you think *that's* bad, you had to go through
Krum to get there! And a few miles the other side of Slidell
was *Drop,* Texas!) Several times I've used this as an illustration of conformity:

I figure the Devil is as smart as the people who make Chev-
rolets. Well, every year the Chevy folks come out with a
"new" model. It may not be much different from last year's
model, but at least the chrome's been shifted around, the
shape may be slightly altered, and there are bound to be a
few gimmicks added. So now it's *this* year's car! People like
that; they want to be "up to date." (Don't get me wrong
—Chevrolet *is* constantly improving their fine car—but naturally, it's not totally new every year.)

Well, now . . . the Devil knows all this too. He knows
we like to be "up to date." So he comes out with a "new
model Sin" every year! Oh, they're the same old sins, all
right, but they LOOK different! They're modern! And
brother, if he can get you to believe that "everybody's doin'
it" . . . you're hooked! That's conformity.

Conformity has been called "the sin against freedom itself." After all, what do we need *freedom* for, if all we do do
is imitate the guy next door? Might as well be a noodnik or
a zombi! What *you* need to be is—YOU!

I admit that to spring away from conformity takes courage.
But you've "got what it takes." Youth has a certain Rebel
quality that can be used for good things.

Here's an example. You've heard of the old college fraternity Hell Week? And the headlines—"Boy dies of blood poisoning after fraternity initiation . . ." . . . "Youth seriously injured in hazing . . ." Yet it's gone on and on just because fraternities have "always done it" and no one had either the inspiration or the courage to change the pattern. THEN, a while back, along came an athlete at Indiana University named Bob Lollar, pledge trainer for Alpha Tau Omega. Bob watched some young pledges wearing freak hair-cuts wasting a lotta manpower pushing empty wheel barrows around the campus, or moving piles of stones from one place to another and back again.

Well, Bob decided that considerable brains and brawn were being frittered away. He went to the smart young assistant dean. He asked, "Isn't there some constructive job for my pledges to do? *Why not make Hell Week—Help Week?*"

They found jobs to do, plenty of 'em. Lollar's twenty pledges painted the Christian Center (a drab old building used by half a dozen churches). A list of other projects were compiled. Other fraternity chapters joined the movement. Within a few weeks the whole campus was alive with useful activity. They cut and stacked wood for a widow with five kids, isolated on a farm. They roofed the home of a family bogged down by illness. They painted the city band-stand, cut grass in the park, rehabilitated a Boy Scout camp. The idea spread to other mid-west colleges—Purdue, Butler, Bowling Green—then Cornell and colleges south and west.

But at Indiana, Help Week has become universal and the townspeople in Bloomington think there's some sense in "these wild fraternity kids, after all."

Was Bob Lollar, who started all this, "just a do-gooder"? No, Bob Lollar was a young fella with the courage to break a tradition that went back almost to the founding of fraternities. And what gave him the idea? Well, Lollar was a veteran when he started at Indiana. And to a man who had been through *real* Hell, "Hell Week" seemed silly. And Bob felt that the idea of conforming to a crazy tradition, just because "everybody did it," would have been worse than "silly." It would have been un-American.

Here's a real good yardstick to use. Is "what everybody's doing" in the crowd, or the town, right? Is it right for *you?* Is it right for *America?* If so, fine. If it isn't—well, somebody's got to kill that Conformity virus, before it becomes an epidemic!

You're the doctor! And you can do it!

A famed atheist came through a small Midwestern town many years ago. He was on a lecture tour, and had converted many weak people to atheism. He had destroyed their faith and left them no hope at all for the Eternity that lies ahead for all of us. He was a powerful speaker, with a keen mind and booming voice.

All the people in this small town had heard of the speaker and turned out to hear him in the big High School auditorium. He hadn't spoken long before it was obvious that a great many in the packed, hushed auditorium were surrendering to the force of his oratory and his misguided "logic." As the evening went on, an objective news reporter who was in the audience said that "you could feel the faith of these townspeople drifting out of the hall, like a fog in the noon sun."

But just as the orator was winding up his lecture, somewhere in the back of the hall a very young girl stood up, and in a trembling voice began to sing, "Stand up, stand up for Jesus . . ." Her mother, tears coming to her eyes, stood beside her and joined in the song. An aged man, then a whole family, and suddenly the whole assembly was on its feet, and the music of their voices shook the old auditorium! The great atheist, looking somehow very old and tired, bowed his head and went his way, the song still ringing in his ears.

Don't *you* be a "chicken!" Stand up for what you know is right. Be a leader, not a follower! If *we* can all be strong, Uncle Sam will always be as wealthy and successful as he is today. And more important, America will always be free!

11

Brains vs. Bombs

I read a horrifying story in the *New York Times* recently. It was fiction, and dealt with the world's last survivors. These Americans lived deep in the earth, in an area called Depth 7. Their living quarters, prepared for the inevitable H-bomb war, had become their tomb. The war had occurred, as expected, and now a heavy blanket of lethal radiation lay over the whole surface of the earth. Not a living soul moved on the earth, or in the six levels above Depth 7. The people living in this last stronghold of humanity would *never see daylight again!* Their children would be born, grow up, and die, never having seen the sun or the moon!

As I said, this was obviously fiction. But friend, it *could* come true! And in your lifetime, too. This brings us to Ed Murray's third main Challenge to Youth—1960!

It's the challenge: *TO AVOID NUCLEAR WAR.*

It makes me sick in my soul that young people today have this threat hanging over their heads. Why can't you grow up in a carefree, happy existence the way God meant you to? Well, you can't, so remember, being *realistic* is part of being mature, and I think we need all the mature young people we can lay hands on these days.

Now, what can *you* do to help America answer this giant challenge. We've talked already about how you can help us beat Russia in peaceful competition. And for two chapters,

we've looked at ways you can help keep our country strong
in every way.

Now there are a couple of other things you can do. Fight
fear! Think positively!

Quit saying, "War is inevitable!" (That is, if you've been
saying it.) This doesn't mean to pull the ostrich bit, and bury
our heads in the sand, pretending that there's no danger. But
as David Sarnoff said, "We've left the vocabulary of confidence and victory to the other side."

Look, we *invented* positive thinking! Norman Vincent
Peale may have come up with the name, but we've been practicing it since this country first ran up the flag of independence. Remember, God has always been on the side of right
and freedom. So when you hear somebody trying to spread
doom, put 'em down! The Communists would love to scare
us right out of our pants, 'cause if our knees were knocking
loud enough, we'd never hear 'em sneaking right up behind
us 'til they said, "Guess who?"

So be active. Be positive. Have faith in God and our leaders. And there's one other Very Important Way you can help
guard against nuclear war in the future.

Start a Chain Reaction in Your Brain:

A big Southern high school has come up with a new slogan
—"It's Smart to Be Smart!" I heard about it while I was ap-
pearing in Atlanta last Spring. The kids in that school down
yonder have begun to put a big new emphasis on brain power.
All I can say to them and their slogan is a loud and fervent,
"Amen!"

You don't have to be from Parentsville these days to realize
(as we've said) that *education is a vital weapon* in the competition between Democracy and Communism. Obviously
—the smartest side is gonna win!

And the smartest side is going to be the one with the most
education!

And, right this minute, *you* are lapping up this valuable Brain Food.

So it looks like whether you're "smart enough to be smart" is of World Shaking Importance. Right? Right.

Boy, I'm tellin' you, I wouldn't have missed out on high school and college, for anything in this world! I just *knew* that my life couldn't be as much fun, or as successful, or as worthwhile, as it would be after I'd soaked up some knowledge. Most of my buddies and gal friends felt the same way. Not all of 'em, though.

Good ol' Jimmy Ford (I hope he won't sue me for using him as an example) was a popular guy in high school. He graduated when I did, and was one of the very few who didn't go right on to college. Instead, he joined the Marines. When he came out, all his buddies were 'way ahead of him in college, so he hopped a bus to Chicago and went to work in his brother's gas station. He never had minded hard work, and pretty soon he was doing well enough financially that when an opportunity came to open his own station, he was able to take it. It happened that he was located on a very busy street, and with long hours and plenty of elbow-grease, Jimmy built up a very profitable and successful business. Not long ago, he drove into Nashville in a shiny big car that had his old buddies' eyes poppin'!

Do I hear someone saying, "See? Who needs an education? I can do OK without it!" To which I reply, "Sure—you might." Just *might*. But you haven't heard the end of the story yet. Guess what Jimmy's doing now? He's going to night school!

He still wants that college education! He told me that in spite of the fact that he had money and a reasonably secure future, he felt he'd been gypped. He didn't feel he was really what he could be, as a person. I'm proud of Jim, for goin' ahead and doin' it the hard way!

Don't you rob yourself of your brightest future! The new, *new* look is brains before brawn!

Tony Marvin, to me, is living proof of this fact. When I was a regular on the Arthur Godfrey show, I noticed a strange thing about Tony. On each of the Wednesday night shows, there was usually a "study or den" set . . . a place where Mr. Godfrey sat while he explained what was going on during the show. On TV, it looked as if Mr. G. was in his own den or library at home. Now on the bookshelves behind his desk there were rows and rows of old books. They were volumes that had been bought from dealers who were stuck with them. In other words, they were the kind of books nobody reads.

But Tony would *read* them! On almost every break, I'd see Tony pull one of the books out . . . at random . . . and begin to skim through. He read with great interest, and lovingly put them back in place when he was through. Sometimes I'd sneak over and see what kind of book he'd been so interested in . . . it'd be an old medical journal, a Treatise on Hives in Warm Weather, a handbook of electronics . . . anything! Tony just got a kick out of learning. It was fun to be smart!

For that matter, I've never met *anybody* who has such an unlimited range of interests as Mr. Arthur Godfrey himself! Why do you think he can hold millions of people spellbound for hours on end, year in and year out? Because he knows little bits about a million things, and is constantly "recharging his battery," broadening his horizons. He loves it!

In just a very short time, America will hand to you the job of AVOIDING NUCLEAR WAR! And the best way to handle that is to start a chain reaction in your brain *right now* . . . and as that reaction spreads to the 18,000,000 young minds of today, as education wakes up those 18,000,000 "sleeping giants" behind those crew-cuts and pony-tails, new strength will flow into Uncle Sam's veins.

And brother, when a really fit, alert, and educated America flexes it's muscles, that Russian bear had better head for the hills!

12

Pilgrim Fathers— Pilgrim Sons

I'm a showman—Junior grade. I've already learned to save the biggest and the best for the last. So here's my closing number—the fourth and final challenge that starts with birth and never stops:

THE PERSONAL CHALLENGE, THE CHALLENGE OF EACH MAN TO THINK AS CLEARLY AS HE CAN AND CHOOSE THE RIGHT COURSE OF ACTION, THE HIGHEST VALUE, FOR HIMSELF.

As you can see, this covers all the others like a blanket. We've been facing it one way or another ever since we started this book-chat. It's what life is all about—and we're back where we started from—with the Importance of Being You!

It may not leave you laughing, but, as we put down our Coke bottles, tidy up, snap off the light, and say good-bye, it should leave you with a lot to think about—and maybe something worthwhile to remember me by.

We'll meet again, of course, and when we do we'll probably be singing, or laughing, or yakking it up—but what will make us *real* friends is that we'll have shared these last, most serious moments together, looking at the Great Questions that face every free man or woman—'twixt twelve and twenty —'twixt thirty and forty—and 'twixt fifty and ninety:

What shall I do with my life?

What should I do for myself?

For my neighbor?

For my family?

For my country?

For the world in which I live?

I can't answer 'em for you. Wouldn't want to if I could. You'll have too much fun answering 'em yourself.

But I have had fun trying to pass along a few helpful tips. If you've found 'em useful I hope you'll look around and pass 'em on to somebody else.

Are you "your brother's keeper?" Don't let anybody fool you. You are—should be. People often quote this line from the Bible as if a "brother's keeper" was a *bad* thing to be. They forget that it was what Cain said to God after he'd slain his brother, Abel. God wanted Cain to tell him where Abel was and Cain said—in effect, "How should I know? Am I his keeper?"

And as God drove him out to wander, alone and branded for the rest of his days, His answer rang out for all eternity— "YES—YOU ARE!"

Professor William R. Parker of the University of Redlands once said, "The best you can do is *start* as your *brother's keeper,* grow into your *brother's helper,* and eventually become your *brother's brother.*"

I suppose that if I didn't feel drawn to you like a brother, I wouldn't have taken time out from Cooga Mooga's TV rehearsals, from recording, from movies, from my little brood in Teaneck and a million other things that crowd into my days, to have this chat with you. But I feel a closeness to you, in many ways. You've written the letters that brought all this on. You've bought the records and seen the movies and watched the TV shows . . . in other words, you've put me on stage. Now the least I can do is tell you how it happened, and try to help you into your *own* private spotlight!

We've talked about You, your talents, your ambitions. About how to get along with the other folks in your life. About your love and your eventual marriage. About your place in this old world, and your importance to it. You probably didn't think I *meant* it when I said I'd show you how YOU could have a big influence on the whole world . . . right now, today . . . did you? Well, I think I've showed you. Now it's up to you.

You're facing into some big challenges. You've got some big decisions to make. And there's one last tip I have to give you. It's the most important of all.

The greatest, most exciting, most thrilling thing in this whole life is to discover that, so long as we're trying, we're *never alone,* and *we have all the help we need at every single second of time!*

What do I mean?

I mean that God, Himself, is our "ever present Help" in trouble, "our Strength," our "Fortress," our "Comforter." Christ walks with us every step of the way if we let Him, if we put our hands in His and follow His instructions.

And this is the most exciting *adventure* of all!

How do I know this?

Two ways. I've read the promises in the Bible. And I've proven it in my own life. Let me explain.

The Nose Cone And The Steeple:

I was asked by the teen reporters if I thought "the steeple is being replaced by the nose cone"—or if God is losing ground in the Space Age.

Why, I *must* answer—How could it? How could He?

I think as we begin to look into space, to contemplate trips to the moon, to be more and more familiar with the other planets—we've just *got* to say, "What a fantastic set-up this is!" It couldn't have been an accident! It *has* to be the hand of GOD behind this show—creating, sustaining, keeping the whole unbelievable watch-works ticking!

Without Him it's all a little too much for us—to put it mildly. When you stop to think that if the sun were just a little closer, *we'd all roast alive*—or if it were just a little farther away *we'd all freeze*—it doesn't take too much faith to accept God as the Being who keeps things adjusted!

The problem is: will you take time in this busy, rush-rush age, to make Him a personal friend—to get to know Him well enough and learn His instructions thoroughly enough so that you can *Prove His Reality* and *Power* for yourself?

Boy, have I been lucky! I've had the greatest pair of parents anybody ever had, the finest environment to grow up in, the best schooling, the most wonderful friends, and many, many laughs and good times on the way. But, best of all, while I was just a child I came to know God.

Y'see, my family and I are members of the Church of Christ. All good members of the Church read the Bible regularly. We know something of the teachings of Jesus when we're very, very young. And as we grow older, we're taught to "prove what He can do in our lives."

And I've done it! I told you once about the time I lost my brand new Official League baseball, when I was around 13. My buddy Milford Smith and I had seen approximately where it landed, but the grass was tall, and we just couldn't spot it. Mama was calling to me to come home, and brother, she *meant* it. I felt that if I didn't find it now, I never would —and yet my time had run out. We'd looked all over, anyway.

But just as I was to leave, the realization flashed across my mind that God could help me if He wanted to! Quickly, I closed my eyes right there and asked Him to help me find my baseball . . . and when I opened my eyes, *it was the first thing I saw!*

This was the first of many such evidences that God is real, and will help me (and you) in little difficulties, as well as the Big Challenges and Decisions that face us all.

The most recent evidence happened while I was in Venice, Italy, last spring, taping a TV show for our Chevy series here. An urgent decision had to be made. It concerned a movie role, the lead in a very big, important film. All I had to do was to say "Yes" and the deal was set. But for a reason that I can't explain to you, I didn't feel I could conscientiously play the character involved.

Morally and spiritually, my instinct told me "No." And yet I couldn't quite come to a decision. So much was involved . . . millions of dollars in the production, a new dimension to my acting career, perhaps even my future in the movies!

I placed a call from Venice to Nashville, Tenn., to my old friend, Mack Craig. I've always valued his judgment, and I felt he could help me. But the cables were busy and the call was delayed. Later in the day, several American ministers of the Church of Christ in Italy dropped by from their respective towns to say hello. I told them the situation, and asked their help.

They were a little hesitant to make a decision, too. One of them, Kenneth Beard from Padova, suggested that we go up to my hotel room and pray about it. After all, it was a moral and religious matter—mightn't we expect God to help us make up my mind? We quickly agreed, and went up to my room together.

We'd been praying for just a minute or two, when the phone began to ring. Naturally, we tried to ignore it, but the ring became more insistent. Finally, prayer was interrupted and I walked over and picked up the phone.

It was Mack! He'd finally been put through to me. I told him my problem, and after a few moments' discussion, we came firmly to the decision that I would be wrong to play the part. Even as I hung up the receiver to tell the others of the decision, I wondered why it had been so difficult!

Later, it hit me that I couldn't have *had* a more immediate and direct answer to my prayer than that annoying, insistent telephone's ringing. It brought the advice I needed, and thus the answer to our prayer! *You* might call it coincidence. I don't.

Wise old Solomon, in his Proverbs, said: "Keep thy heart with all diligence, for out of it are the issues of life . . ." *all* the issues.

And so, my good friend, my last and very earnest piece of advice: to begin to meet this personal challenge I'd really recommend above everything else—that you *go to church regularly, study the Bible instructions and promises, and make prayer a real part of your life.* (Prayer being, as we've said, our point of contact with this Great Power we know as —God.)

Religion is not much good if it's something you put on like a Sunday suit, or a Sunday dress. It has to become a way of life, backed by all your energy and enthusiasm, if you want to prove its reality and the "ever present Help," "Strength," "Comfort," "Joy," and "Abundant Life" that the Bible promises.

You never outgrow it, either.

Burton Coffman, minister of Manhattan Church of Christ (where I worship in New York), told me that some visitors were *stunned* the other day when he invited them to Sunday School. "Why, we thought Sunday School was for *children!*"

Burton set 'em straight in a hurry, and showed them to their class the following Sunday. No, you're never too old to feel the need for God in your life. And you're never too big, too busy, or too important!

Soon after the good ship *Mayflower* dropped anchor, close to Plymouth Rock, William Bradford wrote of its passengers: "They knew they were Pilgrims . . . so they *committed themselves to the will of God and resolved to proceed,*" from which statement they drew their title "Pilgrim Fathers," as well as leaving us a record of the source of their strength.

I had my "ears lowered" about three hours ago. When I dropped the fee into Rudy the Barber's hand, I "committed" our country to God, because it says on the coins in my pocket, on the dollar bills you and I spend—"In God We Trust." Well, don't we?

Remember Mr. McKown's social science class? Well, his kids boiled, but didn't explode until his "pretend propaganda" stomped on their freedom to *worship!* That's because this nation exists, and can *only* exist, as we say each time we pledge allegiance to our flag—"Under God."

C'mon, let's you and I, repeatedly and consciously and prayerfully place our nation "under God." Ask him to help us—He *will!*

It seems to me the very greatest thing they could say about YOUR generation would be—"they knew they were Pilgrims . . . so they committed themselves to God and resolved to proceed."

Then you'd be the Pilgrim Sons of the Pilgrim Fathers— and the Lord would walk with you every step of the way to meet and win every challenge facing you and your world, today and tomorrow and every day.

Well, that's it. We're through. Have fun now. Laugh a lot, think a lot, work a lot. Enjoy each day, each minute, as it comes—and make the most of it.

I'll keep on singing, 'till you get tired of the Boone noise. But whether that day comes or not, I hope you'll keep the Welcome Mat out for me—as a buddy—from now *on.* There's always a little light in the window of my heart for you.

Don't forget that your life is not just yours alone. A lot of people in this old world are counting on us, on you and me. I have a hunch we're not gonna let 'em down.